A Great Mystery

Peter J. Leithart, *A Great Mystery: Fourteen Wedding Sermons*
Copyright © 2006 by Peter J. Leithart

Published by Canon Press, P.O. Box 8729, Moscow, ID 83843
800-488-2034 / www.canonpress.org
Printed in the United States of America.

Cover design by David Dalbey.
–Front cover image "gift with a note," Hadi Djunaedi, 2006
  Used under license from Shutterstocks, Inc.
–Back cover photography by Mark LaMoreaux.
  (From top to bottom: Luke & Rachel Jankovic, Megan Leithart,
  Mark & Kristen Beauchamp, and Kristen Beauchamp)
–Back cover illustration by Alisha Dalbey. (Matt & Ana Dau)

06 07 08 09 10 11   9 8 7 6 5 4 3 2 1

Library of Congress Cataloging-in-Publication Data

Leithart, Peter J.
  A great mystery : fourteen wedding sermons / by Peter J. Leithart.
     p. cm.
  ISBN-13: 978-1-59128-037-8 (alk. paper)
  ISBN-10: 1-59128-037-0 (alk. paper)
  1. Wedding sermons. 2. Marriage--Sermons. I. Title.

BV4278.L45 2006
252'.1--dc22
                                                        2006007303

A GREAT MYSTERY

FOURTEEN WEDDING SERMONS

by

Peter J. Leithart

CANON PRESS · Moscow, Idaho

To
Garnett Pierce Leithart

CONTENTS

PREFACE

ONCE UPON A TIME, staying married was simply what everyone did. It took no more energy or determination than it does to avoid drowning while sitting in a boat carried along by a lazy river. You just had to stay put, careful not to rock back and forth, and the current would do the rest. The destination was perhaps not marital bliss, but it wasn't marital catastrophe either.

Over the last half-century, this lazy option has vanished. Nearly a decade ago, in her book *The Abolition of Marriage*, Maggie Gallagher concluded that marriage was over as a legal institution:

> From a formal, legal standpoint, marriage is no longer an enforceable commitment. The legal, social, and economic supports that sustained marriage over centuries have been dispatched with astonishing speed, and marriage has been reconceived as a purely private act, not a social institution. . . . Thanks to no-fault divorce and the attitudes, norms, and policies that support it, getting married now more closely resembles taking a concubine than taking a wife.

The various ferments that cluster under the umbrella of "the Sixties"—feminism, the sexual revolution, changes in divorce laws—are usually blamed for the demise of marriage, but these are only the most overt and visible and recent enemies of marriage. The more serious threats are those that go unnoticed either because they have so thoroughly triumphed in the erotic imagination as to become invisible as the air or because they have been around long enough to attain a kind of venerability. Edifices of great antiquity can certainly topple quickly, but only when they have been rotting for a long time.

Here I will mention only two of the many deeper and longer-term factors that have conspired to soften the foundations of marriage in modernity. The first is what Zygmunt Bauman has described as the "liquidity of life" in late modernity. In our consumption-obsessed society, everything has become a "commodity," that is, a good used *up* in the using of it. A china tea set is not a commodity; a styrofoam cup is. Goods are commodified when they are purchased with an implicit "use by" date. In part, this universal disposability is driven by technology and the marketing that accompanies it—your kids want the newest X-Box when it comes out, because there will be games that cannot be played on the old console. In other sectors, the speed of change has more serious consequences. No matter how secure his position may seem, the computer programmer who fails to keep up will suffer more than shame; he'll be out of a job. In late modernity, the chameleon flourishes, and the market favors the Protean being that is capable of a self-makeover at a moment's notice.

Social relations tend to get caught up in the drive toward commodification. As Bauman says, the modern world "privileges those who can travel light," and therefore "if changed circumstances require a fast move and starting anew from scratch, long-term commitments and any ties difficult to untie may prove to be a cumbersome burden— ballast that needs to be thrown overboard." The sexual lives of high school and college students suggest that social connections have been thrown into hyperdrive. "Going steady" and even "dating" are becoming outdated, replaced by shifting alliances that last a night or a weekend. All the pathologies of contemporary marriage—high divorce rates, serial polygamy, the trophy wife—are perfectly consistent with the way we live, with the one overarching imperative to *keep up*. The current has quickened, and there are ample opportunities to skip from boat to boat. If you go with the cultural current, this is where it takes you. To *stay* married, by contrast, is to stand against much that the contemporary world holds dear. When the whirl rules, persistence in a permanent commitment is an act of the most profound subversion.

The second cultural force that has undermined traditional marriage is the romantic conception of love, which is largely the product of the late eighteenth and early nineteenth centuries. Distortions are more difficult to identify here. Erotic passion did not spring into existence two centuries ago, and passion has always been a recognized enemy of obligation, especially marital obligation. The romantic conceptions of love, furthermore, owe a significant debt to the semi-Christianized notions of the medieval courtly love tradition. Without the confession that God is love and that God has saved the world out of love, what Robert Polhemus has called "erotic faith" would never have taken cultural hold. Yet, the erotic faith of romantic love is a threat to Christian love and marriage, since it represents a substitute for Christian faith.

As Polhemus describes it, erotic faith is

> an emotional conviction, ultimately religious in nature, that meaning, value, hope, and even transcendence can be found through love—erotically focused love, the kind of love we mean when we say that people are in love. . . . Men and women in the hold of erotic faith feel that love can redeem personal life and offer a reason for being. . . . with the spread of secularism since the eighteenth century, erotic faith, diverse and informal though it may be, has given to

some a center and sometimes a solace that were traditionally offered by organized religion and God. By love we can
change the situation—that sentiment moves people: love
relationships have the highest priority in the real lives of
millions as they have had for innumerable characters in
fiction.

Love at first sight is the sacrament of erotic faith—a love
that is not merely sexual attraction but, as Anthony
Giddens puts it, "an intuitive grasp of qualities of the other.
It is a process of attraction to someone who can make one's
life, as it is said, 'complete.'"

The flaw in this romantic conception is subtle but deadly.
The key shift can be neatly expressed as a grammatical one,
a shift from the Christian confession that we love because
we are first loved to the erotic faith in first love, or love at
first sight; from the Christian confession that the God of
love saves to the erotic faith that Love saves; from the Christian confession that God is love to the erotic faith that Love
is god. The faith that self-transcendence and "completion"
come through erotic attachment to another human being
is a species of idolatry. Marriages built on or infected with
this vain hope are doomed, for what happens when the satisfaction is lacking, as it must be?

To resist these cultural tides, Christians need both a practical understanding of marriage and an understanding practice of marriage that is rooted in something deeper than
mere moral exhortation. We need a marital understanding
and practice rooted in the reality of the living, triune God
of love. Hence this brief collection of wedding sermons,
which I would somewhat playfully call a "systematic theology of marriage."

I didn't set out to write a systematic theology of marriage. I wrote each sermon individually, attempting to offer a meditation that was relevant for the couple and bringing into play my fascination *du jour*. When I had finished
a dozen or so sermons, I realized that they were beginning

to form a set of approaches to theology from the perspective of marital love— for each locus of systematic theology can be illumined by images drawn from marriage. The perichoretic union of Father, Son, and Spirit can be unpacked in terms of the one-flesh union of man and woman (cf. 1 Cor. 6), a one flesh that under God's blessing produces a "third" that serves as a site where the love of the two meets. Barth was surely at least partly right in saying that man is the image of God precisely as he is male and female, in the differentiated unity of sexuality. Adam's fall was his failure as a guardian-husband, and Israel's history could easily be allegorized as the story of a marriage (Ezek. 16). In Jesus, God and man are united as One, which is another echo of the one-flesh marital relation, as the Eternal Word came to dwell in the feminine flesh of humanity. Jesus came as the bridegroom who offered Himself for His bride, the Church, which is sustained through history by the bridal washing of baptism (Eph. 6) and the continual celebration of the Lamb's marriage supper. Believers are "one spirit" with Christ as man and woman are one flesh (1 Cor. 6). The history that began with the glorious bride revealed to the risen Adam in the garden will end when a heavenly bride descends from heaven to be face-to-face with her new Adam forever.

Trinity and anthropology; original sin, covenant and call of Abraham; Christology and pneumatology; ecclesiology, sacramental theology, eschatology: they are all there for those who have eyes to see, tightly wound in, with, and under the daily round of a common bed, sex, conception, childbirth, and childrearing, conversation, work, and mutual comfort. For those with eyes to see, the mystery of marriage is the mystery of the world, and those with such eyes might be able to recognize and avoid the shoals that lead to marital shipwreck, the rocks toward which every cultural trend drives us.

*　　　　　*　　　　　*

I would like to thank all the couples at whose weddings I delivered these sermons, both for the privilege of uniting them as husband and wife and for permission to use their names in this collection. Thanks also to Doug Jones at Canon Press for his interest and willingness to publish it, and to Jared Miller for planing rough spots in my prose.

This book is dedicated to my fourth daughter, Garnett Pierce. Born when my wife and I were in our mid-forties, Garnett feels like our first granddaughter, her brothers treat her like a favorite niece, and all the kids have great fun calculating how old they will be when Garnett graduates from high school. At two, she is, I trust, a couple of decades away from marriage, but when one reaches a certain age decades begin to pass as minutes once did, and so I am beginning to brace myself for that inevitable walk down the aisle. My confident prayer is that when that day arrives she will be firmly rooted and grounded in the triune love of the God in whom she already lives and moves, and that she will spend a long life bearing fruit like a tree beside the waters.

1 DIVINE LIFE

Marriage of Daniel and Khiree Appel
May 18, 2002

SCRIPTURE READING

Genesis 1:24–28; 2:18–25

Then God said, "Let the earth bring forth living crea-
tures after their kind: cattle and creeping things and beasts
of the earth after their kind"; and it was so. God made the
beasts of the earth after their kind, and the cattle after their
kind, and everything that creeps on the ground after its
kind; and God saw that it was good. Then God said, "Let
Us make man in Our image, according to Our likeness;
and let them rule over the fish of the sea and over the birds
of the sky and over the cattle and over all the earth, and
over every creeping thing that creeps on the earth."

God created man in His own image, in the image of God
He created him; male and female He created them. God
blessed them; and God said to them, "Be fruitful and mul-
tiply, and fill the earth, and subdue it; and rule over the fish
of the sea and over the birds of the sky and over every living thing that moves on the earth." . . .

Then the LORD God said, "It is not good for the man to
be alone; I will make him a helper suitable for him." Out
of the ground the LORD God formed every beast of the field
and every bird of the sky, and brought them to the man to
see what he would call them; and whatever the man called
a living creature, that was its name. The man gave names
to all the cattle, and to the birds of the sky, and to every

beast of the field, but for Adam there was not found a helper suitable for him. So the LORD God caused a deep sleep to fall upon the man, and he slept; then He took one of his ribs and closed up the flesh at that place. The LORD God fashioned into a woman the rib which He had taken from the man, and brought her to the man. The man said,

> "This is now bone of my bones,
> And flesh of my flesh;
> She shall be called Woman,
> Because she was taken out of Man."

For this reason a man shall leave his father and his mother, and be joined to his wife; and they shall become one flesh. And the man and his wife were both naked and were not ashamed.

HOMILY

All the world over, the beginning of a marriage is marked by celebration and festivity. Even in an age when divorce is rampant, when millions of children grow up in broken homes, when families consisting of his, hers, ours, and somebody else's are the norm—even in our day, weddings continue to possess an atmosphere that belies the facts of contemporary marriage. Think of the energy expended on the preparations for a wedding—not just this one, but any wedding. Think of the joy and expectation that fills not only the couple but also the family and friends. Think of the care and attention given to every last detail of the service.

That last point is especially striking. Pastor Wilson remarked to me yesterday that weddings are the last bastion of formality in an age of informality, the last ritual in a culture barren of ritual. Though we punctuate almost nothing else with ceremony, and "winging it" is the order of the day, weddings are still written in italics, underlined, and bold-faced.

Why is this? What is it about marriage that elicits such effort, joy, and hope? Why do we lavish so much attention, time, and expense on weddings? Why, even in the most unceremonious civilization in history, do we still turn weddings into ceremonies? Why, in a culture where spontaneity reigns everywhere else, is a wedding the one event that is still scripted?

In part, we make ceremony out of a wedding because we recognize that this event marks a decisive transition in the lives of everyone present. That is most obvious in the case of the couple: Daniel and Khiree came into this room as single people, from opposite sides of the room; they came in as two *Is*, but they will go out together as a married couple, as a *we*. An hour ago, there was this one and that one; less than an hour from now, two will be made one.

But the transition is not just a transition in the histories of the couple, but also in the lives of their families and friends. Daniel's and Khiree's parents will remain parents, but after today, they will never again be parents in the same way that they have been. Daniel and Khiree will still have siblings, but those relations will change as well. Friends will remain, but those friends will from this day be dealing with a couple—not just with Daniel, but with Daniel-who-is-married-to-Khiree; not just with Khiree, but with Khiree-who-is-married-to-Daniel.

Weddings mark a death and resurrection. For everyone here, one world ends today and another world begins; everyone dies today and everyone is risen. Death and resurrection is a miracle, a great mystery too full of wonder and danger to meet head-on, and so we feel safe in approaching it only through the indirection of ritual.

Behind this, however, is something more fundamental. When we address this question as Christians, we realize that weddings continue to have this hold on us because at a wedding we have a glimpse of the inner story of human history. History is the story of a marriage, beginning with Adam awaking from a deep sleep to find Eve, through Satan's seduction of Eve at the tree of knowledge, through Jesus awaking from death to see the women come to the garden tomb, to the final revelation of the bride at the end of all things, the bride-city that surrounds her Husband and is filled with His glory. As Jonathan Edwards put it, the Father created a world so that His Spirit could prepare a bride for His Son. Marriage is the alpha and omega of human history. Even pagans have some sense of this, recognizing that a wedding unveils some vast secret.

But I think we need to go further than this, and Edwards points the way. Weddings provide a glimpse not only of the meaning of all human history, but also of the meaning behind the meaning of human history. At a wedding, and in a marriage, we can see through the dark glass and glimpse, however briefly and dimly, the life of God.

The Bible teaches that marriage is a covenant relation: a binding, personal relationship that demands love, loyalty, and faithfulness from all parties. That is what you, Daniel and Khiree, are entering today, by the marriage oaths that you will make in a few moments. And that covenant relationship pictures the relationship of Jesus Christ and His bride. But beyond that, it pictures the relationship of the persons of the Trinity. Father, Son, and Spirit constitute the original, the eternal covenant community, an eternal fellowship of love, loyalty, faithfulness.

In fact, it's only because God is triune that marriage is possible. Since the world is created by a triune God, the world is not made up of unrelated individual things, nor is it simply one big thing. Since the world is created by the triune God, the creation, like God Himself, is a harmony of difference, a dance, polyphony. Because God is triune, it is possible to make a *we* from two *I*s, to make a *we* where each *I* remains an *I*.

Marriage forms a union that reflects the inner life of God. God is Father, Son, and Spirit; the Father is God, the

Son is God, and the Spirit is God; yet the Father is not the Son, the Son is not the Spirit, the Spirit is not the Father, and there are not three gods but one God. So in a marriage, two are united into one and yet remain two. As we've read, "God created man in His own image, in the image of God He created him; male and female He created them." The image of God is located in Adam and Eve as individuals, but it is also located in their union with each other. In this primordial human society of husband and wife, we have the first image of the God who is an eternal society.

Yet the triune character of marriage is not just a philosophical point, and marriage is not some mathematical or metaphysical puzzle. Instead, the Trinity shows us the basic shape of marriage. Paul tells us in various places that the marriage relationship pictures Christ's relationship to His church, but in 1 Corinthians 11:3, he says that marriage pictures the relation of the Father and Son: "Christ is the head of every man, and the man is the head of a woman, and God is the head of Christ." The Father's headship over Christ is the archetype of the husband's headship over his wife.

Since we're sinners, we get this all wrong. Men hear that they are heads of their wives as God is head of Christ, and all they hear is that they get to live like gods. We think we have an excuse to act like little tinpot deities around the house, spending our lives enthroned in the easy chair, holding the channel-changer as a scepter, demanding beer and chips. "I'm like God to my wife, after all," we say. Women hear that their husbands are godlike heads over them, and they wonder, "Why does he get to play God, while I have to slave around?" They conclude they can only be like God if they can wrest headship from their husband.

Both these conclusions are wrong because they assume and proclaim a false view of God. When a husband hears that his relation to his wife is like God's headship over the Son, and he uses that as an excuse to tyrannize and dominate his wife, he is saying that the Father is a tyrannical despot over His Son. When a wife hears that she has to submit and concludes that her dignity has been destroyed, she is saying that the Son can have honor only if He usurps the place of the Father. In both cases, they are giving false testimony about the character of the Trinity. Both the domineering husband and the grudgingly submissive wife are committing blasphemy.

The God revealed in Christ is no tyrant, no dictator. He is the Giver of every good and perfect gift, who gives to all without reproach, who shines His sun on the righteous and the wicked. And He is the *eternally* giving God; before all worlds, the Father was glorifying the Son through the Spirit, and the Son was honoring His Father through the same Spirit, and the Spirit was enfolding both in glory, light, and love. God is, and is essentially, the God who gives Himself. Christ gave Himself in love for His bride, and this self-sacrifice of the incarnate Son reveals the eternal character of God. Christ gave Himself for the life of the world not *in spite of* being God, as if self-giving contradicted the nature of God; Christ gave Himself *because* He was God. To live divinely is to live as gift. Self-giving is the shape, the dynamic, the choreography of divine life.

Both husband and wife are called to live lives patterned after the life of God. Husbands are to love their wives as Christ loves the church, and also as the Father loves the Son. Husbands are properly heads of their wives only if they imitate the Father's loving headship over Christ. Wives submit to their husbands as the church to Christ, and also as the Son glorifies and honors His Father. A marriage formed by the pattern of the Trinity will be simply this: The husband, like the Father, giving himself in every way to beautify and glorify his bride; the bride, like the Son, giving herself at every opportunity to honor and glorify her husband.

Discerning the trinitarian pattern of marriage gives us a hint of the life of God, but it also places a demand on those who are married. Self-giving does not come naturally to fallen men and women. Self-indulgence is much easier than self-denial; forcing others to sacrifice for you is far more the norm than sacrificing for another. Especially in a marriage, you are called to self-denial. A marriage without self-denial and self-giving is destined to be a disaster.

And so, this is my charge and exhortation to you both: Through Christ, you both have been brought into the eternal fellowship of Father, Son, and Spirit. By the grace of God, live divine lives together; strive by the grace of God to make your marriage an image of your Creator. Daniel, offer yourself every day to glorify Khiree, who is your glory; Khiree, offer yourself every day to glorify Daniel, who is your head. And may your marriage not only bring you both great joy, but may it radiate divine life and love and power, so that everyone you meet will know from your marriage that you serve the Father of Jesus Christ, the giving God, the God who is gift.

In the name of the Father, and of the Son, and of the Holy Spirit. Amen.

2 ELECT IN LOVE

Marriage of Aaron and Katy Cummings
October 11, 2003

SCRIPTURE READING

Isaiah 61:10–62:5

> I will rejoice greatly in the LORD,
> My soul will exult in my God;
> For He has clothed me with garments of salvation,
> He has wrapped me with a robe of righteousness,
> As a bridegroom decks himself with a garland,
> And as a bride adorns herself with her jewels.
> For as the earth brings forth its sprouts,
> And as a garden causes the things sown in it to spring up,
> So the Lord GOD will cause righteousness and praise
> To spring up before all the nations.
> For Zion's sake I will not keep silent,
> And for Jerusalem's sake I will not keep quiet,
> Until her righteousness goes forth like brightness,
> And her salvation like a torch that is burning.
> The nations will see your righteousness,
> And all kings your glory;
> And you will be called by a new name
> Which the mouth of the LORD will designate.
> You will also be a crown of beauty in the hand of the LORD,
> And a royal diadem in the hand of your God.
> It will no longer be said to you, "Forsaken,"
> Nor to your land will it any longer be said, "Desolate";
> But you will be called, "My delight is in her,"

And your land, "Married";
For the LORD delights in you,
And to Him your land will be married.
For as a young man marries a virgin,
So your sons will marry you;
And as the bridegroom rejoices over the bride,
So your God will rejoice over you.

Revelation 21:2–5a

And I saw the holy city, new Jerusalem, coming down out of heaven from God, made ready as a bride adorned for her husband. And I heard a loud voice from the throne, saying, "Behold, the tabernacle of God is among men, and He will dwell among them, and they shall be His people, and God Himself will be among them, and He will wipe away every tear from their eyes; and there will no longer be any death; there will no longer be any mourning, or crying, or pain; the first things have passed away." And He who sits on the throne said, "Behold, I am making all things new."

John 2:1–11

On the third day there was a wedding in Cana of Galilee, and the mother of Jesus was there; and both Jesus and His disciples were invited to the wedding. When the wine ran out, the mother of Jesus said to Him, "They have no wine." And Jesus said to her, "Woman, what does that have to do with us? My hour has not yet come." His mother said to the servants, "Whatever He says to you, do it." Now there were six stone waterpots set there for the Jewish custom of purification, containing twenty or thirty gallons each. Jesus said to them, "Fill the waterpots with water." So they filled them up to the brim. And He said to them, "Draw some out now and take it to the headwaiter." So they took it to him. When the headwaiter tasted the water which had become wine, and did not know where it came from (but the servants who had drawn the water knew), the headwaiter called the bridegroom, and said to him, "Every man serves the good wine first, and when the people have drunk freely, then he serves the poorer wine; but you have kept the good wine until now." This beginning of His signs Jesus did in Cana of Galilee, and manifested His glory, and His disciples believed in Him.

HOMILY

At the beginning of his letter to the Romans, Paul describes himself as a "bond-servant of Jesus Christ, called as an apostle, set apart for the gospel of God" (1:1). By the last phrase "gospel of God," Paul was not merely saying that the gospel originates from God. He was saying too that the gospel is *about* God—about God's righteousness, His love, His mercy, and His grace. The good news is that God is not like the harsh gods, nor like the indulgent idols of our imaginings. The good news is that God is like the Father of Jesus, that God is like Jesus Himself. No, the gospel is more: The good news is that the Father of Jesus *is* God, and that Jesus Himself *is* God made flesh. The good news is that God has revealed His character and His purposes in His Son. The gospel is no gospel without the incarnation; there is no good news without the good news of Christmas. According to this gospel of God, the words of Jesus are the words of God, the compassion of Jesus is the compassion of God, the death of Jesus is the human death of God the Son, and the resurrection of Jesus is the victory of God.

A wedding is a public, ceremonial display of the gospel, and the marriage that follows a wedding is a continuing proclamation of the gospel. The gospel is not a "religious" addition to marriage; it is of the essence of marriage. Every marriage displays the gospel, whether faithfully or unfaithfully, whether a true gospel or another gospel. Confusion about the gospel always produces confusion about marriage and family, and vice versa. And since the gospel is the gospel of *God*, confusions about God are always reflected in damaged and dysfunctional marriages.

How is a wedding, how is a marriage, a proclamation of the gospel of God? There are many ways to express this, but I want to highlight two. First, the gospel announces that God will be among us, and that He will make His home in us. From all eternity, the three persons of the triune God have dwelt with each other and have made their dwelling *in* each other. The Father dwells in the Son by the Spirit, and the Son dwells in the Father by that same Spirit. The Word that is with God and is God has always been in the "bosom" of the Father. The gospel announces that the Father has room in Himself for us, that He opened Himself to be our dwelling place, our high tower, our refuge and home. The reverse is also true, for through the Spirit and Son, the Father comes to dwell within us and make us His home. John saw this in his vision at the end of Revelation: "Behold, the tabernacle of God is among men, and He will dwell among them, and they shall be His people, and God Himself will be among them" (21:3).

A healthy marriage proclaims this truth of the gospel of God. In a healthy marriage, the husband is the fortress, refuge, and home of his wife, and the wife is a refuge and home for her husband. This is symbolized sexually, when the woman becomes a bodily dwelling for her husband, even as her husband surrounds her in a loving embrace. In the Song of Songs, the lover and the beloved describe each other as gardens of delight; each is a place where the other can frolic in joy. "I went down to the orchard of nut trees," the lover says, "to see the blossoms of the valley, to see whether the vine had budded, or the pomegranates had bloomed" (6:11). His beloved responds: "Like an apple tree among the trees of the forest, so is my beloved among the young men" (2:3).

Sexual union embodies the aspirations of your marriage as a whole. You are called throughout your lives, in every aspect of your lives together, to be dwelling places for each other. Aaron, by your vows, you are promising to open your life—your resources, your body, yourself—as a place where

Katy may dwell securely; and Katy, you are promising that your life and your body is Aaron's home, and his alone. And by opening yourselves to one another, you will also be opening yourselves to become dwelling places for still others, for children and for friends and for the fellowship of the saints. By maintaining the intimacy of that fellowship, and as your love for each other overflows in children and ministry, your marriage will provide a glimpse of the intimate communion of the Trinity and proclaim the gospel of God.

This is difficult, even impossible for us. Our natural, sinful instinct is to close ourselves to one another, to treat others as obstacles to our own plans and programs. We don't want people to "dwell within" us, and we don't care to "dwell within" each other. How many marriages end precisely here, with a husband and wife who dwell under one roof but do not in any significant way dwell in each other, where husband and wife are closed off, each dwelling in the suburbs of the other's good pleasure? Aaron and Katy, you can only realize the intimate sharing that your marriage calls you to through the power of the Spirit, who has made a home for us in God, and who opens us to one another. Only if God dwells in and with you by His Spirit do you have any hope to dwell in and with one another. Or, to change the analogy: Your marriage will be truly harmonious only if, by the Spirit, it is a variation on the three-voiced fugue of the triune fellowship, the three-voiced fugue that *is* the triune fellowship.[1]

My second point is that the gospel reveals God as a God who *chooses*, a God who *elects*, a God who singles out a Bride for His Son and in His Son. It's been said that "the doctrine of election is the sum of the Gospel because of all words that can be said or heard it is the best: that God elects

---

[1] These reflections on the ethics of perichoresis are inspired by an article by Khaled Anatolios, "Divine Disponibilité: The Hypostatic Ethos of the Holy Spirit," *Pro Ecclesia* 12, no. 3 (Summer 2003).

man; that God is for man too the One who loves in freedom."[2] God is eternally and necessarily love, for Father, Son and Spirit freely and completely loved one another from eternity to eternity. Yet before the foundation of the world, before God spoke the first word of the creation, He had chosen to be God *with* His people. He has elected to be a God who rejoices over His people as a young man over his bride. He has elected to devote all His infinite resources to being God *for* us. God, who is free and in need of nothing, has determined that He would not be God without His people.

At every Christian wedding, this good news of God's election is being acted out. Aaron and Katy, today you are declaring your choice of one another, and you are covenanting together to formalize that choice. Aaron, you are vowing today that you will not be Aaron unless Katy is at your side, and Katy, you are vowing that you will not be Katy without Aaron. Your promises to one another are a display of the gospel of election. And, as God seals His bride with an anointing of the Spirit, so you are sealing your mutual choice and mutual possession by anointing one another. This choice to be with—and refusal to be without—each other is the nature of every covenant. A covenant is not a contract; a covenant is not merely an exchange of gifts. A covenant is an exchange of persons. By your covenant vows, you are electing to *be* only if you can be *with*, and be *for*, one another.

The election that is formalized today has to be worked out every day of your marriage. Even Yahweh, the perfect Husband of Israel, met with rejection and rebellion. Yet He remained steadfast in His choice. Every time Israel was called "Forsaken" or "Desolate," God made sure that this was not the final word. After the words "Forsaken" and

---

[2] These are the words of Karl Barth, *Church Dogmatics*, Vol. 2, Part 2 (Edinburgh: T. and T. Clark, 1958), 3.

"Desolate," God spoke the words "Married" and "My delight is in her." After every "No," God, the electing God, had determined that He would continue to say "Yes."

Aaron and Katy: Proclaim the gospel of God by being faithful to your choice through every difficulty and disappointment, through every loss and trial. As you both know, it is entirely possible for a marriage to preach a false gospel. It is possible for a marriage to say that God is *not* faithful, that His calling and election *are* revocable; it's possible for a marriage to say that God may tire of His bride and seek out another. You are called by your oaths today to proclaim the truth about God in your marriage, to live every day of your marriage in the light of today's anointing. You have elected to be one flesh; persist in that choice, be faithful to that election, so that nothing but death can separate you.

In the Name of the Father, and of the Son, and of the Holy Spirit. Amen.

3 THE BEGINNING OF ALL BEGINNINGS

Marriage of John and Naomi Lewis
May 10, 2003

SCRIPTURE READING

Genesis 1:1–2

In the beginning, God created the heavens and the earth. The earth was formless and void, and darkness was on the surface of the deep, and the Spirit of God was moving over the surface of the waters.

OPENING PRAYER

Lord God, Creator and Sustainer of all things, who formed Adam from the dust of the ground and Eve from a rib taken from Adam's side, be present here today, we pray, and be at work to form this man and this woman into husband and wife. Guide our meditations as we consider the beginning of this new marriage and this new household, for the sake of Jesus Christ, who lives and reigns with the Father and the Spirit, one God, age after age. Amen.

HOMILY

A wedding is a beginning, a day of creation. John and Naomi, today you are leaving behind your old homes and starting a new one; today you are embarking on a new life as a married couple; today you'll be given new names, the names of husband and wife. This is a day of beginnings, not only for the two of you but for all your family and friends. For them, too, after today nothing will be quite the same as it has been. As in the original creation, this beginning occurs because of God's action, because of the power of His word. Pastor Wilson will pronounce the words, and you will hear his voice, but his voice is accomplishing what the Word accomplished in the original creation. Through him, God is taking hold of you; God is giving you new names; God is settling you into new patterns.

This is a day of beginnings, but all beginnings are dangerous and problematic in many ways. In these few moments, I want to reflect on some of the problems of beginnings.

Many people are afraid to begin. In part, this is because of the uncertainty of the new, but there is also a deeper, subtler reason for this fear. Beginnings, in our experience, always tear. A sermon or a speech begins by tearing through the silence that preceded it; a child is born only by opening a breach in his mother; a new political or religious movement is only recognized as new when it has torn away from the movements that came before—otherwise, it is just more of the same old thing. In making the world, God took hold of the creation and tore it into pieces before He assigned names and pronounced it good. At the initiation of every covenant, animals were torn and burned on the altar. At the beginning of the beginning of the new creation, the heavens were rent as the Spirit descended on Jesus, and at the end of the beginning of the new creation, we see the torn flesh of the crucified Son and the temple veil ripped from top to bottom. At the beginning of this new Lewis household, John and Naomi are being torn from parents and siblings, and the fabric of everyone's life is being unraveled.

We think that only endings tear: "How could he have been torn from me?" asks the grieving widow. "I feel I've been ripped in two," says the divorcee. "They might as well strip the skin and flesh from me," says the man betrayed by lifelong friends. Endings do tear. But if we stop with that, we are still thinking like children. Maturity recognizes that this is only half the story; maturity recognizes that beginnings can also leave their wounds. Maturity recognizes that the feeling that everything is coming to an end and the feeling that everything is just beginning are often the *same* feeling. Maturity recognizes the inner unity of death and birth.

So, one problem of beginnings is this: If beginnings tear and possibly wound, why begin? Why try anything new? Why go through with the challenge of forming a new household if it means tearing up the old one? Why not bear the ills we have rather than fly to others that we know not of?

Some fear beginnings; others fear that beginnings are impossible. Stuck in the rut of frustrated career expectations or a disappointing marriage, many people long for nothing more than a new start. But they live with the horrifying conviction that it cannot happen. "Where did things go wrong?" they ask themselves. "If only I could go back to that instant and do it differently. If only. But you can't turn back the clock," they say. "And a man can't be born again when he is old, can he?" these Nicodemuses ask. And they mean it as a rhetorical question. This is a second problem of beginnings: The fear that we can never begin again.

And what are beginnings anyway? We're always in the middle of things, always surrounded by realities that have already begun, always in the midst of circumstances over which we have no control and which we did not originate. Aren't beginnings just arbitrary constructions of human minds and human language? When did World War I start? With an assassination? With the formation of the armies at the first battle? With the first shot? With the first casualty? With the assassin's secret decision that today is the day? Isn't isolating one single "beginning" a fiction? Or, to the matter at hand, when did John and Naomi begin to love one another? Can either of you isolate the moment? Was it the poem she recited to the rhetoric class in her freshman year? Was it the theological question he asked in Lordship class? Was it the glance he gave during a choir rehearsal? Or did it begin on some bright, unremembered afternoon in junior high when Naomi first saw the Texas flag and secretly vowed, in a way that even she does not completely understand or recall, that she would someday marry a Texan?

Beginnings are difficult, even impossible, to locate. By the time we ask where we began, we have already begun. And that becomes a severe problem when we recognize that how our lives go forward and how our lives end are bound up in our beginnings. Beginnings set the course for what follows. Without Aristotle or Freud, there would be no Aristotelians or Freudians. But at the same time, beginnings authorize what follows; beginnings *limit* what follows. Once Aristotle had written his treatises, being an Aristotelian meant certain things and excluded others; to be an Aristotelian meant to talk about substance and accidents rather than Oedipal complexes and the superego. When John decided to pursue Naomi, he simultaneously decided *not* to pursue the hundreds of other women he knew or might come to know in the future. Every decision we make is a beginning, and each of these beginnings sets us out on a journey in a particular direction toward a particular end. We seem to be slaves to our beginnings. But when and how did we begin?

This is a third problem of beginnings: The more we inquire, the more beginnings elude us; airy nothings, they melt into air, into thin air. And yet, our lives in whole and in their parts are lived out within the confines set by beginnings; our beginnings conspire with our ends to lock us into a confining *inclusio*. And so we may be overshadowed by the fear that our lives are governed and controlled by a nameless, faceless something that we can never discover or understand. We are slaves to our beginnings, but our beginnings evaporate at the slightest glance. And that seems like the worst kind of tyranny.

For us as Christians, these problems of beginnings are addressed by the first sentence of the Bible. Genesis 1:1 says without any equivocation that there was once a beginning, and if there was once a beginning it follows that there can also be a new beginning. We know that the answer to Nicodemus's question is yes—a man can begin again when he is old, if he is born of water and Spirit. Even death is not an end, for it is swallowed up in the victory of resurrection.

But there is another point in Genesis 1:1 that is equally important. The opening words of Genesis, "In the beginning God," are true not only of the beginning of the creation; these words are true of all beginnings. Believing that God is Creator is more than believing He started things off some thousands of years ago; by itself, that is Deism, not Christianity. To say God is Creator is to say that He is the Beginning behind every beginning. It should be no surprise for us that the search for beginnings is like futilely exploring an endless cavern, for at the beginning of every beginning we come face to face with the God who is without beginning. Yet, the Beginning is neither nameless nor faceless. His Name is Father, Son, and Spirit, and we see His face in the face of Jesus. This means that what appears to be slavery to our beginnings is not really slavery, and that the limitations which beginnings impose are not really limitations. For without the "confinement" of beginning, we would not be at all, and without the limitation of beginning, there would be nothing to limit. The fact that God is Creator of each and every circumstance does not make Him a tyrant. Because He is Creator of each and every circumstance, His beginnings make our freedom possible—for where the Spirit of the Lord is, there is liberty.

I said earlier that beginnings, in our experience, are marked by tears. But Scripture begins with an account of a beginning, of *the* beginning, in which the key actors are the Word and Spirit of God. In fact, Word and Spirit are always at work at the beginning of things, and always at work moving things toward their conclusions. In particular, the Spirit is active in the week of creation, ordering and furnishing the world, and He is present at all other beginnings. When the Spirit is poured out on a devastated land, it is transformed to a garden; the Spirit stands as a witness at Sinai, comes down as a dove upon the New Adam, and is poured out for the Church's rebirth on the day of Pentecost. Wherever there is a beginning, there is the Spirit; wherever the Spirit is, there is a new beginning.

Yet, the Spirit of beginning initiates without tearing—and where there are tears and wounds, the Spirit binds up those wounds. The Spirit of beginning, the Spirit who was from the beginning and is without beginning, this Spirit begins from the Father without tearing from Him, and returns from the Son without tearing from Him. This Spirit is the gift of love that *binds* Father and Son in eternal communion; the Spirit sets the rhythm of the life of God, an eternal dance of beginning and ending and beginning again. And when the Spirit enters the world to initiate it and move it to its conclusion, He continues to dance by the same steps. In the creation account, when the sword of the Word has torn heaven and earth asunder and the Word has torn the seas so that dry land appears, the Spirit binds the tattered pieces into a new and more glorious tapestry and establishes a world that is ever again new. And through this Spirit the torn body of the crucified Son is restored in the body of His resurrection. The Spirit who stands at every beginning is the Spirit who *binds* rather than tears, who heals every wound, who closes up every breach.

I'll end where I began: John and Naomi, today is a beginning for you, and everything I've said about beginnings applies to what you are doing here. At every point, you can follow through faithfully only if you rely wholly on the continuing work of the Spirit, the Spirit with whom you began.

Do not be like the Galatians, who began by the Spirit but sought then to be perfected by the flesh.

Today's beginning, like all beginnings, sets you off on a particular course. The words you will speak place *limits* on the way you may live in the future. You are committing yourself to a kind of bondage today, chaining yourselves to one another. From this day on, you are accountable for loving and caring for one another in every circumstance, as long as you both shall live. But these are limits only in the sense that choreography limits a dancer's movements; so long as you keep in step with the Spirit, the limits of this beginning will enable you to live a free and joyous life together.

By the words you speak and the words Pastor Wilson speaks today, your world will be torn. Things will never again be the same; that is the nature of a beginning. But if you walk by the Spirit, the world you have known is being torn only to be put back together into a pattern more wondrous than you can yet imagine.

And this will happen not just today. Your life as a married couple will be a series of endings and new beginnings, until death finally tears you from one another. You can face this future with confidence only if you rely on the Spirit of Jesus, the Spirit who transforms every end into a fresh beginning, the Spirit who is not the God of the dead, but the God of the living, the God of the living again.

CLOSING PRAYER

Almighty God, heavenly Father, You are without beginning and without end. You are the Beginning behind all our beginnings, and You enclose all our beginnings and all our endings in the embrace of Your Word and Spirit. We pray that Your Spirit would hover over the waters again to form a new household here today, and we pray further that Your Spirit would dwell in that house and in both John and

Naomi from this day forward, until we come to the beginning of the day that is without end. We pray through Jesus Christ our Lord, who lives and reigns with you and the Holy Spirit, ever one God, age after age. Amen.

4 DIVINE EROTICS

Marriage of Brendan and Sharon O'Donnell
July 2, 2004

SCRIPTURE READING

Isaiah 62:1–5
> For Zion's sake I will not keep silent,
> And for Jerusalem's sake I will not keep quiet,
> Until her righteousness goes forth like brightness,
> And her salvation like a torch that is burning.
> The nations will see your righteousness,
> And all kings your glory;
> And you will be called by a new name
> Which the mouth of the LORD will designate.
> You will also be a crown of beauty in the hand of the LORD,
> And a royal diadem in the hand of your God.
> It will no longer be said to you, "Forsaken,"
> Nor to your land will it any longer be said, "Desolate";
> But you will be called, "My delight is in her,"
> And your land, "Married";
> For the LORD delights in you,
> And to Him your land will be married.
> For as a young man marries a virgin,
> So your sons will marry you;
> And as the bridegroom rejoices over the bride,
> So your God will rejoice over you.

OPENING PRAYER

Almighty God, our heavenly Father, who out of Your great love sent Your Son to a desolate and forsaken world to rescue His bride and to rejoice over her with singing: Draw near to us through Your Spirit, we pray, and fill us with wisdom, joy, and thanks as we consider the love You have shown to us in Your Son. We pray this in the name of Jesus our Lord. Amen.

HOMILY

Scripture is clear that marriage is a sign and image of the mutual love that exists between Christ and His church. This is explicit in Ephesians 5, where Paul instructs husbands to "love your wives as Christ also loved the church and gave Himself up for her." In Paul's mind, the parallel is very strong. He quotes Genesis 2:24 ("for this cause a man shall leave his father and mother, and shall cleave to his wife, and the two shall be one flesh"), but then goes on to clarify that, despite appearances, he is not talking about human marriage but about Christ's marriage to the church.

But what kind of love does Christ have for His bride? What kind of love is marriage supposed to incarnate? What kind of love is your marriage, Brendan and Sharon, supposed to manifest?

Greek has several words for love: *philia*, which refers to friendship and brotherly affection; *agape*, often defined as self-giving, selfless love; and *eros*, often defined as self-love or self-seeking love. *Eros* and *agape* have often been sharply contrasted. In the words of Alan Soble, "*Eros* is acquisitive, egocentric or even selfish; *agape* is a giving love. *Eros* is an unconstant, unfaithful love, while *agape* is unwavering and continues to give despite ingratitude. *Eros* is a love that responds to the merit or value of its object; while *agape* creates value in its object as a result of loving it. . . . *Eros* is an ascending love, the human's route to God; *agape* is a descending love, God's route to humans."[1]

On this account, if I love with agapic love, I love without regard for any satisfaction or pleasure that might come to me: agapic love is the love of the Good Samaritan for the victim on the road to Jericho, the love of the martyr for his persecutors, Jesus' love for sinners. If my love is erotic, I want at least to be loved in return, and I seek all the satisfactions and pleasures, often including sexual pleasures, that accompany requited love. Erotic love is the love of the courtly lover struck by the arrow of desire, the love of a thousand romantic films and novels, the love of the Platonic mystic who ascends from beautiful things to the contemplation of Beauty itself, the love that hopes to own what it loves. Erotic love seeks possession; agapic love freely dispossesses. Erotic love is self-seeking; agapic love is pure love for the other. Erotic love often seeks physical satisfaction and verges dangerously close to lust; agapic love is spiritual. In the minds of many Christians, Christian love aims to be thoroughly agapic.

Not surprisingly, this contrast of *eros* and *agape* creates deep tensions in the Christian understanding of marriage. On the one hand, Christ's agapic love for the church sets the pattern for a husband's love for his bride, but on the other hand, marital love is irreducibly erotic. Isn't marital love always self-seeking to some degree? Don't husbands and wives, quite naturally and rightly, desire to be loved? Is marital love in the end doomed to be a corrupt or even perverse image of the true love of the Divine Bridegroom for His bride?

Some Christians address this dilemma by offering a more favorable assessment of *eros*. C. S. Lewis agreed that there is a "carnal" element in erotic love, but he refused to accept

[1] Alan Soble, *Eros, Agape, and Philia: Readings in the Philosophy of Love* (New York: Paragon, 1989), from the introduction.

that *eros* could be reduced to sexual desire, much less reduced to lust: "Very often what comes first is [not sexual
desire but] simply a delighted pre-occupation with the Beloved—a general, unspecified pre-occupation with her in
her totality. . . . If you asked [a man under the influence of
eros] what he wanted, the true reply would often be, 'To go
on thinking of her.'" Lust is quite different: "We use a most
unfortunate idiom," Lewis says, "when we say, of a lustful
man prowling in the streets, that he 'wants a woman.'
Strictly speaking, a woman is just what he does not want.
He wants a pleasure for which a woman happens to be a
necessary piece of apparatus." *Eros*, by contrast, "makes a
man really want, not a woman, but one particular
woman."[2] In this view, *eros* responds to the good, true, and
beautiful in the beloved, and that means that Christ's pro-
hibition of lust is not an attack on *eros*, but the opposite.
It is a tragedy that "erotic" has come to be synonymous
with "pornographic." Christian condemnation of lust is, as
John Paul II has argued, an appeal for a "true eroticism,"
a desiring love that does not reduce the beloved to a sexual
object but is attracted to the image of divine goodness and
beauty in the person loved.

To this extent, Brendan and Sharon, you are called to
express erotic love in the whole of your marriage. This
eroticism, in fact, is at the heart of the vows you are taking today. You have committed to keeping yourselves only
for one another so long as you both shall live. This is not
merely a pledge of sexual faithfulness, though of course it
is that. Brendan, you have promised to be preoccupied, not
with "a woman" but with Sharon, and Sharon, you have
pledged to delight not in "a man" but in Brendan. By your
vows today, you are setting out on the adventure of discov-
ering and celebrating in each other the refulgence of God's

[2] *The Four Loves* (San Diego: Harcourt Brace Jovanovich, 1960),
chap. 5.

glory that is the image of God; you are committing yourselves to discover and celebrate that radiance in ever fresh
ways so long as you both shall live. You are called, in short,
to "true eroticism."

Yet, a basic question remains. Erotic love seeks for satisfaction and therefore appears to be self-interested. But
God can receive nothing and hopes to receive nothing from
us, and yet He loves us. *Eros* seems completely absent from
God's love for His bride, so how can you manifest God's
love in your marriage?

The answer is simple: God does desire us, He longs for
us, He considers us His lovely and spotless bride, and He
does look for a response. God's love for us is erotic, for He
takes interest in each of us and loves us in order to evoke
love from us. God's love includes His desire to be loved. We
must feel the full weight of this truth. The triune God is
eternal, and He is eternally full of all joy, love, fellowship,
feasting, and life. He needs nothing, and nothing that He
makes can add even in a smallest degree to the satisfaction
of the triune fellowship. And yet, this same God created a
world and called it good; this same God assures us that He
delights in His world and His people. Through the prophet
Isaiah, Yahweh says that His exiled people will no longer
be called "Forsaken," but instead, "you will be called 'My
delight is in her' and your land 'Married.' For as a young
man marries a virgin, so your sons will marry you; and as
the bridegroom rejoices over the bride, so your God will
rejoice over you" (Is. 62:4–5). And again, "I create Jerusalem for rejoicing, and her people for gladness. I will also
rejoice in Jerusalem, and be glad in my people" (Is. 65:18b–
19a). The prophet Zephaniah says of Jerusalem, "Yahweh
your God . . . will exult over you with joy, He will be quiet
in His love, He will rejoice over you with shouts of joy"
(Zeph. 3:17). And Jesus Himself says that the Father sent
Him because the Father out of love "seeks worshipers" who
will worship in Spirit and in truth (Jn. 4:23–24). That such

a God would rejoice over us is, as Paul would say, a great mystery, but it is true.

What makes marital love a true image of divine love is not the renunciation of desire; rather, what makes love truly love is the kind of desire it expresses and the kind of response it anticipates. True *eros* desires a particular kind of return: a return with difference. A true exchange of love is never an exchange of identical items. As David Hart says, "A gift that is exactly reciprocated is a gift that is returned, rejected . . . a tautologous return of the same, a violence, like a blow instantly returned."[3] Had Sharon given Brendan the exact ring Brendan gave her, the message would be "The engagement is off." To hope that you will receive exactly the same love you give is the crudest form of self-love. You might as well gaze longingly and affectionately into a mirror. All givers give in hope of a return, but a return with difference; every lover hopes his beloved will reciprocate his love, but the wise lover knows that the reciprocated love will be as wonderfully different as the beloved herself. And the wise lover joyfully embraces that difference, even as he joyfully embraces his beloved.

Don't lose sight of this in your marriage. Brendan, you are called to love, and it is right for you to want Sharon to love you. But Sharon is not called to give back exactly what you give her. If you want only what you can give, you might as well stay single and live with a bunch of guys for the rest of your life, or march off to live by a railroad track. Sharon is a woman and will love you as a woman, which is not, I need hardly remind you, the way you love. Likewise, Sharon, you are pledging today to give yourself in love to Brendan, and you do that hoping and wanting him to give himself to you. But do not expect him to give back exactly what you have given him, for he will love you as a man, and

---

[3] *The Beauty of the Infinite: The Aesthetics of Christian Truth* (Grand Rapids: Eerdmans, 2003).

not just a man; he will love you as only Brendan can. Once again, this means you are both called to express true *eros*. "True eroticism" is, Lewis says, "a delighted preoccupation" with each other, and true eroticism is a delighted preoccupation with the otherness of each other.

And in this, too, you are displaying the love of God, the eternal love of the Father, Son, and Spirit. For the Father pours out His love on the Son and Spirit, and He desires the Son and Spirit to love Him in return. And they do, but to the Father's joyous paternal love the Son returns something surprising and fresh; the Son returns filial love. To the love of the Father and Son, the Spirit returns the love that only the Spirit can give. To the melody of the Father's song, the Son and Spirit respond not by repeating the melody, but with harmonious counter-themes. Brendan and Sharon, as you love and as you hope to receive love from each other, as you give and reciprocate with delighted surprise in your differences, you will be imitating the love of God, the eternal round of love that is both *eros* and *agape*, the eternal polyphony of love that is yet beyond both.

In the Name of the Father, and of the Son, and of the Holy Spirit. Amen.

5 NAKED AND UNASHAMED

Marriage of David and Alisha Dalbey
September 25, 2004

SCRIPTURE READING

Genesis 2:25; 3:7

And the man and his wife were both naked and were not ashamed. . . .

Then the eyes of both of them were opened, and they knew that they were naked; and they sewed fig leaves together and made themselves loin coverings.

OPENING PRAYER

Almighty God our Father, we praise You for Your Son Jesus Christ, our Husband and Lord, the Author and Perfecter of our faith, who for the joy set before Him endured the cross, despising the shame, and has sat down at Your right hand in heaven. Enable us to lay aside every encumbrance, and the sin that so easily besets us, so that we might run with endurance the race that is set before us. Through the same Jesus Christ, who lives and reigns with You and with the Holy Spirit, ever one God. Amen.

HOMILY

David and Alisha: Today, you are entering into the covenant of Christian marriage. David, you are swearing in

God's name that you will love Alisha as Jesus loves the church and gave Himself for her. You are promising with an oath to give your life for her sake. Alisha, you are swearing in the name of God to submit to David with joy, love, and fear, obeying him as the church submits to Christ and obeys Him. You are becoming one flesh, and you are called to work out that unity in your daily life as husband and wife. David, you are called to be Adam, and Alisha, you are called to be Eve. And together you are called to make your home a small restoration of Eden. The covenant you make today calls you to a level of devotion, sacrifice, love, and self-giving that you have never yet attempted or experienced. You are entering unexplored territory. And as you cross this threshold, it is important that you understand something of the challenge of the promises you are making.

The two verses I've read point to a central problem that every marriage has faced since the Fall of Adam. Prior to the Fall, Adam and Eve were naked, exposed to God and to each other, and yet experienced no shame. After the Fall, things are radically different. Adam and Eve recognize that they are naked, and throughout Scripture, shame and nakedness are closely linked. When the Lord threatens to judge His faithless bride Israel, He says He will shame her by exposing her nakedness: "I Myself have also stripped your skirts off over your face, that your shame may be seen" (Jer. 13:26). In some prophetic passages, nakedness is associated with the shame of defeat and enslavement: "the king of Assyria will lead away the captives of Egypt," Isaiah says, "young and old, naked and barefoot . . ., to the shame of Egypt" (Is. 20:4). Genesis 3 does not say that Adam and Eve were ashamed after the Fall, but it does say that they recognized their nakedness, and in the Bible that is as good as saying that they were ashamed.

Besides, they act in all the telltale ways that humiliated people do. They are fearful, as Adam explicitly confesses to Yahweh: "I heard Your voice in the garden, and I was afraid because I was naked" (3:10). Their sense of naked exposure before God leads to isolation from God: Because he is afraid, Adam says, "I hid myself" (3:10). Adam's shame not only expressed itself in his relation to God, but in his relation to Eve. Confronted with his sin, Adam does not accept the shame, confess it, and seek reconciliation. Instead, he attempts to deflect the shame from himself to his wife, making her a scapegoat who will bear his shame: "The woman whom Thou gavest to be with me, she gave me from the tree, and I ate" (3:12). Adam and Eve were created to be one flesh, to express in bodily form the unity that exists among the persons of the Trinity. Sin brought shame, shame brought fear, and fear brought isolation. Shame means exposure, and Adam reacts to his exposure by attacking his wife. Instead of being one flesh, man and woman go to war. And all this arises from shame.

It is no accident that the first institution of postlapsarian culture, the first human invention following the Fall, is clothing. Clothing is the first institution of postlapsarian culture because the shame of exposure, the shame of nakedness, is the first experience of fallen man.

These verses are profoundly relevant to marriage. By its very design, marriage strips away clothing, removes the fig leaves; at its core, marriage means a return to primordial, prelapsarian, pre-Fall nakedness. This is not simply a point about sex. The nakedness and exposure involved in marriage are far broader than the physical nakedness of the marriage bed. As two are made one flesh, barriers are withdrawn, masks are torn away, and the two who are made one stand exposed before each other in emotional and psychological, as well as physical, nakedness. Marriage is by its nature a return to prelapsarian nakedness, but it is not a return to prelapsarian shamelessness. Here is the dilemma and the danger of marriage: David and Alisha, you are going to be exposed to one another in ways that you've never experienced, and you *will* be ashamed.

There are few things as damaging to marriage as shame that is not handled properly. Some results of shame are obvious, as when a man beats his wife because she makes him feel small and stupid. But the more subtle operations of shame are more common, and in some ways more dangerous. A wife tells her friends at a dinner party about her husband's incompetence on the computer; on the drive home the husband lashes out because of the public humiliation. Stung by her husband's anger, the wife withdraws, and after the outburst they don't talk to each other for a week. After a series of such episodes, they start sleeping in separate beds. Exposure begets shame, which begets anger, which begets withdrawal, which begets estrangement. Or, a husband asks his wife when she is going to go on the diet that she's been promising, and the shame of her husband's comments twists her into depression. Or, parents contemptuously and publicly ask their son why he can't do anything right, and by the time he's sixteen he is responding to years of shame with rage and uncontrollable rebellion.[1]

When shame is not handled rightly, the result is a marriage that looks a lot like the marriage of Adam and Eve after the Fall: Husband and wife isolate themselves from one another to escape continual humiliation; they lash out verbally, physically, and sexually in vengeance for the shame they have endured; and they "hide themselves" because they know they are naked, and they are afraid.

So, is marriage possible after the Fall? Is it possible for two people who have been shamed by sin to be exposed to each other in the ways that marriage requires, without the whole thing spiraling into anger and resentment, withdrawal and isolation? Is it possible for two sinners to be one flesh? Is it possible for two shamed people to be naked and not ashamed?

---

[1] Some of my thoughts here are inspired by Michael Lewis, *Shame: The Exposed Self* (New York: Free Press, 1992).

The answer to all these questions is yes. But this yes comes only as the yes of the gospel, the yes that is Jesus, in whom all the promises of God are "yes and amen." Fulfilling, joyful, and productive marriage is possible since the Fall only insofar as husband and wife, naked and exposed before one another, are at the same time clothed, clothed in Christ's righteousness, clothed in glory. And this is possible only because Jesus has been clothed with shame. The Psalms frequently speak of the wicked being clothed with shame, but the man who is most fully covered with shame is not a wicked man but the one Good Man, Jesus Christ. He was stripped naked, beaten, ridiculed, spit upon, nailed to a cross, and publicly executed. He is clothed with shame, and yet He does not open His mouth, does not lash out, does not attack the bride who shames Him, does not fear, does not hide Himself from His Father. And He endures and even despises this shame for the joy set before Him, the joy of resurrection and glory, the joy of union with His bride, which bride we are.

The first institution of postlapsarian culture, of post-Fall human life, was clothing. But fig leaves do not remove shame; fig leaves can only hide shame. Even the cloaks that Yahweh made for Adam and Eve from animal skins did not solve the problem of shame. But (and this is the gospel) the first institution of Christian life, of post-redemption culture, was also clothing, the clothing of glory and beauty that is from Christ, the clothing of righteousness that *is* Christ. This clothing is the only solution to shame, and therefore it is the only basis for a peaceful, vigorous, joyful, fulfilling, and fruitful marriage.

David and Alisha, you are entering new territory today, and you can only succeed in this endeavor by faith. But your faith cannot be just generic confidence that things will turn out all right. If your marriage is to flourish, your faith must be in Jesus Christ; it must be a trust that the Father has clothed you in the Son through the Spirit. That faith is the only way that you can truly be one flesh. That faith is the only way for you to be a new Adam and a new Eve, naked and not ashamed.

In the name of the Father, and of the Son, and of the Holy Spirit. Amen.

6 EVANGELICAL PROMISE, EVANGELICAL COMMAND

Marriage of John and Moriah Barach
June 25, 2004

SCRIPTURE READING

Ephesians 5:1–2, 25

> Therefore be imitators of God, as beloved children; and walk in love, just as Christ also loved you and gave Himself up for us, an offering and a sacrifice to God as a fragrant aroma. . . .
>
> Husbands, love your wives, just as Christ also loved the church and gave Himself up for her.

OPENING PRAYER

Almighty God, who out of Your great love for the world gave Your only-begotten Son, so that whoever believes in Him might have eternal life in the Spirit, illumine our hearts we pray, that we might know You and become imitators of Your ways, as Your beloved children—through Jesus our Lord, who lives and reigns with You and with the Spirit, ever one God, unto ages of ages. Amen.

HOMILY

Marriage customs vary widely and wildly throughout the world. According to ethnographer Arnold van Gennep's

catalogue, the separation of a man and woman from their
families that takes place in marriage can be symbolized by
"changing clothes; emptying a pot of milk and bursting
three berries; cutting, breaking, or throwing away something connected with childhood or bachelorhood; releasing
the hair; cutting or shaving the hair or the beard; . . . remov-
ing jewelry; consecrating one's toys, such as dolls, one's jewelry, and one's childhood dress to a deity; . . . baring the
waist; changing food habits and being subject to temporary
dietary taboos;" and so on.

The formation of a new household is symbolized by
binding the bride and groom with a single cord; wrapping
them in a single piece of clothing or a veil; sitting them in
the same seat; by the bride and groom massaging, rubbing,
and anointing each other; washing each other; even drink-
ing each other's blood. Among some peoples, the bride's
relatives abduct and hide her shortly before the wedding
until the groom can find her and take her back to his own
home; among others, the groom has to fight to take his
bride from her family in a mock battle that sometimes results in serious injuries.[1]

For good or for ill, battles and abductions, cuttings and
breakings, vampirism and massages are not normally part
of our marriage customs. But at the center of most West-
ern wedding ceremonies is a custom that is nearly universal: an exchange of gifts. Our particular custom goes back
to the Middle Ages. During the Christian Middle Ages, as
John Bossy says, "the central rite of spousal consisted of an
exchange in which the father or 'friends' of the bride gave
her to the groom in exchange for a symbolic counter-gift,
known . . . in England as the *wed*," the word from which
we derive our word "wedding." A "wedding" is, etymologi-

---

[1] The details in the preceding two paragraphs are taken from Arnold
van Gennep, *The Rites of Passage* (Chicago: Univ. of Chicago Press,
1960), chap. 7.

cally, a ceremonial exchange of gifts. Despite many changes during the course of the Middle Ages, "the structure of gift and counter-gift, making alliance by exchange, remained in place underneath." And of course it survives today in weddings where the exchange of vows is followed by an exchange of rings.[2]

This is perfectly suitable from a biblical point of view, for in Scripture covenants are often sealed by an exchange of gifts. When they came to the temple to renew covenant by sacrifice, the Israelites were not to appear before the Lord empty-handed. They were to come near to present gifts. When a new king took his throne, his people brought gifts to express submission to him, and kings often offered gifts to their people at the time of accession. When a covenant was made between a king and his servants, the king offered land and the vassal offered service, and kings entered alliances with other kings by exchanging gifts. When Yahweh took up His throne in the tabernacle, the chiefs of all the tribes of Israel brought treasures to acknowledge Yahweh as their liege.

Biblically speaking, as a covenant ceremony, a wedding also involves gift-giving. The laws of Exodus simply assume that the husband will pay a dowry for his bride: "If a man seduces a virgin who is not engaged, and lies with her, he must pay a dowry for her to be his wife. If her father absolutely refuses to give her to him, he shall pay money equal to the dowry for virgins" (Exod. 22:16–17). Whatever the practical benefits of this system, and they are considerable, the symbolic dimension was equally important. A man entered into a covenant-relationship with a woman by giving gifts.

In the context of marriage, exchanging gifts is an expression of love, since every particular gift expresses the self-gift

[2] John Bossy, *Christianity in the West, 1400–1700* (Oxford: Oxford Univ. Press, 1985).

of the man to his bride and of the bride to her husband. As
Paul says in Ephesians 5, we are imitators of God and we
are His children when we imitate the love of Jesus, His Eternal Son, who manifested His love by giving Himself as a sacrifice to make a fragrant aroma. Paul begins his exhortation
to husbands on the same note, telling them to "love your
wives as Christ loved the church and *gave* Himself for her"
(Eph. 5:25). As a ceremony declaring and formalizing love,
it is appropriate that a wedding should put gift-giving at the
center. And reflecting on the character of gifts will clarify
the kind of love you, John and Moriah, are pledging to one
another today.

What makes a gift a gift? For many moderns, Christian
and non-Christian, a gift is only a gift if the giver renounces
any desire for a return gift. A true giver must not even expect or desire a "Thank you," because even that might turn
the gift into a purchase—you are buying gratitude. And this
understanding of what it means to give a gift is closely related to a particular understanding of love. To love truly is
to love without any desire to *be* loved. True giving is disinterested giving, because true love is disinterested love.[3]

Some appeal to Jesus' teaching to support this view of
gifts and gift-giving, and they are partly right (Lk. 6:35).
Jesus did say that we should give without expectation of
return, and that is an essential biblical teaching about gift-
giving. John, if you give to Moriah only when you believe
she can pay you back in full, your marriage will be full of
disappointment. Your love will dissolve into cost-benefit
analysis, and besides, she will never be able to give you as
much as you think you deserve. And, Moriah, if you with-
hold yourself from John until you know he can pay you
back, you are going to be frustrated in marriage as well.

---

[3] In the background of these meditations on gifts is the work of John
Milbank, especially "Can a Gift Be Given? Prolegomena to a Future
Trinitarian Metaphysic," *Modern Theology* 11, no. 1 (January 1995).

"Do good," Jesus says, "and lend, expecting nothing in return." That is an evangelical imperative, and an essential component of a healthy marriage.

But this is only part of the story. After Jesus issues that evangelical imperative, he gives an evangelical promise: "Do good, and lend, expecting nothing in return"; but then Jesus adds, "and your reward will be great, and you will be sons of the Most High" (Lk. 6:35). So we should desire and expect a return on our gifts after all. In fact, we can expect a return that's far greater than what we have given, for Jesus promises that our reward will be "great." When we give in order to receive something from another human being, the problem is not that we are desiring and expecting too much. Quite the contrary, we are aiming too low, expecting and desiring too little.

This evangelical promise too is essential for a healthy marriage. Many wives become embittered against their husbands. They cook dinner every night, clean house, wash clothes, take care of children, and never receive so much as a "Thank you" from their husbands. Many husbands, for their part, become deeply hostile to their wives because they work six days a week and turn over every cent of their paycheck to their wives to spend. Husband and wife share the same resentments: nothing but giving and giving, they both think, without any appreciation or thanks, with nothing to show for all my time and effort. Bitterness and resentment of this sort arise from a single, simple mistake: the mistake of seeking a reward from the wrong direction. Bitterness takes root when we seek a reward on earth instead of trusting that God will give a better heavenly reward; hatred boils up when we seek return from men and not from God. Troubles arise in marriage when husbands and wives are looking for measly rewards from each other rather than "great rewards" from God.

In the first verse of Ephesians chapter 5, Paul calls us to be imitators of God. We do that by imitating Jesus in His self-giving, but in imitating Jesus we are imitating God, the God revealed in Jesus, the God who is Father, Son, and Spirit. This is true because the life of the Trinity is all about giving gifts, about self-giving in love, and about expecting and desiring a return. The Father gives Himself to the Son expecting a return from the Son, and the Son gives Himself back to the Father, with interest. The Father's loving gift and giving love is met by the Son's gift in the Love of the Spirit, so that the Father's gift is returned in the double gift of the Son and the Spirit. This responsiveness, this desire for response, is the delight and life of the Trinity, and in this way, the triune life is love. God is love because God is the giving God. The love of the Trinity is, as David Hart says, "a love always of recognition and delight, desiring all and giving all at once, giving to receive and receiving to give, generous not in thoughtless squandering of itself, but in truly wanting the other."[4]

John and Moriah, if you want to have a healthy and joyous marriage, you must obey the evangelical imperative, *and* embrace in faith the evangelical promise. Not one nor the other alone, but both together. Give to each other without expecting anything in return, but give to each other confident that you will receive a return, trusting that you will receive a "great reward" in heaven. Then you will be imitators of God, the triune God whose life is giving and receiving and giving again, whose eternal joy is the eternal round of giving that is simultaneously and eternally reception and return.

In the Name of the Father, and of the Son, and of the Holy Spirit. Amen.

---

[4] David Bentley Hart, *The Beauty of the Infinite* (Grand Rapids: Eerdmans, 2003).

7 SURPRISING LOVE

Marriage of Josh and Abby Stevenson
March 15, 2003

SCRIPTURE READING

Song of Songs 1:1–4; 2:10–16a; 8:5b–7a
May he kiss me with the kisses of his mouth!
For your lovemaking is better than wine.
Your oils have a pleasing fragrance,
Your name is like purified oil;
Therefore the maidens love you.
Draw me after you and let us run together!
The king has brought me into his chambers.
We will rejoice in you and be glad;
We will extol your love more than wine.
Rightly do they love you. . . .
My beloved responded and said to me,
"Arise, my darling, my beautiful one,
And come along.
For behold, the winter is past,
The rain is over and gone.
The flowers have already appeared in the land;
The time has arrived for pruning the vines,
And the voice of the turtledove has been heard in the land.
The fig tree has ripened its figs,
And the vines in blossom have given forth their fragrance.
Arise, my darling, my beautiful one,
And come along!"
"O my dove, in the clefts of the rock,

In the secret place of the steep pathway,
Let me see your form,
Let me hear your voice;
For your voice is sweet,
And your form is lovely."
"Catch the foxes for us,
The little foxes, that are ruining the vineyards,
While our vineyards are in blossom."
"My beloved is mine, and I am his. . . ."
Beneath the apple tree I awakened you;
There your mother was in labor with you,
There she was in labor and gave you birth.
Put me like a seal over your heart,
Like a seal on your arm.
For love is as strong as death,
Jealousy is as severe as Sheol;
Its flashes are flashes of fire,
The very flame of Yahweh.
Many waters cannot quench love,
Nor will rivers overflow it.

OPENING PRAYER

Come Holy Spirit, Divine Matchmaker; You have joined the eternal Son in holy wedlock to His bride. You are the Spirit of truth; You inspired the prophets and apostles who wrote these Scriptures, and You have promised to lead us into truth. Illumine us as we consider the Scriptures today, and work among us to bind this man and woman together to be one flesh. For the sake of Jesus Christ, who lives and reigns with You and with the Father, ever one God, world without end. Amen.

HOMILY

Every time we speak, we affect ourselves and the world around us for good or ill. Some words, Scripture tells us, are like sparks that ignite a fire which leaves everyone scorched

(Prov. 16:27). Other words are like the fruit from a tree of life, which brings delight, satisfaction, and nourishment to both speaker and hearer (Prov. 12:14; 15:4). Our words never leave things unchanged. We never say "mere words." Every time we speak, we open up new possibilities for the future.[1]

Some things we say, however, open up a vast future. Saying "Good morning" will affect the next few moments or hours or perhaps the day, but only in rare circumstances does "Good morning" change the rest of someone's life. But there are times when we speak, and in so speaking, our lives are changed radically, foundationally, forever. For many of you here, this is such a day. After Josh and Abby speak the words of the marriage oaths, the Renches will have a son-in-law, the Stevensons will gain a daughter-in-law, siblings will gain a brother- or sister-in-law—everyone's relationship with everyone else will be thoroughly rearranged. Above all, you, Josh, and you, Abby, are going to say things today that will never be erased from your record, words that will invariably and necessarily affect you for the rest of your lives. Whether you keep your vows or not, the rest of your lives will be determined by what you speak today. A man who breaks his wedding oath is guilty only because once upon a time he *took* a wedding oath.

If you have any sensitivity to the momentous character of this event and these words, this day might well be terrifying rather than joyful. After all, you can't know what will happen in the next few moments, much less what will be happening forty years from now. Yet you are making promises that bind you until death. Not knowing what will happen tomorrow, how can you make such promises with any degree of hope?

---

[1] The ideas in these paragraphs are drawn from Robert Jenson, *Essays in Theology of Culture* (Grand Rapids: Eerdmans, 1995), chap. 1: "Language and Time."

A common way to handle the threat of the future is to ignore it and pretend that the future can be controlled and predicted. Ancient peoples attempted to discern the future by observing the flights of birds and reading the livers of sacrificed animals. We are far more sophisticated, yet we still live in a culture obsessed with predicting and controlling the future in thousands of ways, large and small—from the ubiquitous Daytimers and PalmPilots to the social science departments in our universities, from the tics and habits of daily speech to the Federal Reserve System, from the planning meetings in our board rooms to the deliberations of the United Nations Security Council. At every level and in myriads of myriads of ways, we attempt to master the future. We behave as if the future is merely an extrapolation of the past and present, and that if we just get enough facts, the future will bring no surprises. We try to round off time, collect it into a manageable pile, graph and confine the future to the open spaces on our calendars.

But we cannot do it; the future stretches out before us, unknown and unknowable. We Christians, though, have some idea of why the future is so unpredictable. The simple reason is that the future is unpredictible because the God who controls the future is alive, and being alive means having the ability to surprise.[2] Dead things don't surprise us; dead people only surprise us if they come back to life. A rock is a rock is a rock; a corpse is a corpse is a corpse. But a bud blossoms into the astonishing surprise of the rose, and an awkward schoolgirl can grow into the most beautiful of women. The world as a whole is beyond our control and events surprise us because they are ruled by a living God, a God who says to Habakkuk, "Look among the nations! Observe! Be astonished! Wonder! Because I am doing something in your days—you would not believe if you were told" (Hab. 1:5), a God who calls on His people to "come, be-

---

[2] This too is a Jensonism.

hold the works of the Lord" (Ps. 46:8) because He has done a "new thing" in the earth (Is. 43:19). The God of the future is a living God, which is to say, a God who is in the habit of surprising us. Trying to control the future is trying to tame God, even to kill Him. He will not be tamed, and He is life.

Because we believe that the living God is the God of all, the God who was and is and is to come, for Christians the future is an adventure not a terror. The future is an adventure, however, because and insofar as we face the future with faith, with confidence that all surprises are the work of a loving and just and living God, a God who makes promises, a God with the power to *keep* His promises. In Scripture, faith always describes the attitude of confidence we take toward an unknown future: Abram became the paradigm of faith because he left Ur for a land he did not know and had not seen, because he hoped against hope that God would raise up a living son from Sarah's dead body. Faith is the substance of things hoped for and the assurance of things not yet seen.

Every time we speak we open up an unknown and unknowable future. And this means that God has constructed the world in such a way that we can speak with confidence only if we speak in faith. That is true of every sentence we utter. But that reality is even more intensely true here, today, with these words. There are only two ways to say "I do" without terror: you must either ignore the weight of what you are doing, or you must say it with faith. Josh and Abby, you are not making these promises because they will enable you to control your future. You should instead be making these promises with the full recognition that you cannot control your future. You can make these promises, and keep them, only if you are also entrusting yourselves to the living God.

I have spoken of surprise as an inescapable part of living in time, living toward the future, living by faith. There is another kind of surprise that I want to speak of briefly. It is true across the board that the future is *never* merely more of the present and the past, that the future is always full of surprise. But the great example of this surprisingness is love. Love is altogether a surprise, but I want to identify three surprises that are inherent in love.

The first surprise of love lies at its origin, in the astonishing fact that we are loved at all. Only the worst lovers believe they are loved for their merits, for their qualities. It is also a poor lover who loves his beloved for her merits. A man may initially be attracted to his future wife by her beauty, but if a man loves his wife only for that, what happens to his love if age and disease devour and twist her? A woman may love a man for his strong sense of responsibility and leadership, but if that is all, what happens to her love if he should get Alzheimer's? However you look at it, love is not about merit. If it isn't ultimately an astonishing, unmerited gift, it is not love. I did not set My love on you, Yahweh told Israel, "because you were more in number than any of the peoples" but "because Yahweh loved you and kept the oath which He swore to your forefathers" (Deut. 7:7–8). In loving Israel, Yahweh was not responding to a difference between Israel and other nations. Yahweh's love *made* the difference between Israel and all the other nations, and that made all the difference.

It is surprising to become the object of love. But it is equally surprising to become a lover. Love comes on us unawares; it grips and takes hold like some power from without and begins to control us. Love seems to be something done *to* us rather than something we choose to do. This is the second surprise of love. Benedick in *Much Ado About Nothing* got it exactly right: "I do love nothing in the world so well as you. Is not that strange?" This is the truth behind all the romantic poems and novels and movies, behind the mythology of the wound of love and love at first sight. This is the truth that has led many peoples to believe that love is a god or goddess. That is an idolatrous distortion, but it is a distortion of something real. Solomon well knew the overwhelming power of erotic passion. At the beginning of his love song, he writes that love is better than wine, not only more intoxicating and thrilling but also more controlling than wine. Throughout the Song of Songs, the passion of the lovers rules them, so they are as astonished at what love does to them as others are at what they are doing. Why is this man leaping on the hills like a gazelle? Because he is eager to see his beloved. Why is this woman desperately searching city streets at night? Because she is longing for her lover. Why the ecstatic joy of the lover and the beloved? Because each is ravished by the love of the other. Solomon expressed the power of love even more strongly at the end of his song, when he said that love is stronger than death, than the waters of the sea, than fire. Even if all the elements conspired together, and even if death joined the conspiracy, Solomon says, their power would bow before the power of love.

Being loved is a gift of surprise. Becoming a lover is a gift of surprise. But there is yet a further surprise, a third surprise of love. Love means giving yourself to another, defining your life and identity through the life and identity of another person.[3] That applies to all sorts of love—the love of parents for children, of friends for one another, and of a husband and wife for one another. These kinds of love differ, but they are all defined by the refrain of the Song of Songs, the chiasm of mutual possession: "I am his, and he is mine." This, like the realization that the future is unknowable, can be terrifying. When we realize that love demands the loss of ourselves, we might fear that our "I" will be dissolved in a "we." But the third surprise of love is a surprise at the heart of creation: He who loves his life shall

---

[3] This description comes from Robert Solomon, *About Love: Reinventing Romance for our Times* (New York: Touchstone/Simon & Schuster, 1989).

lose it, but he who loses his life shall find it. The third surprise of love is that losing yourself in a "we" makes you all the more yourself, that self-emptying becomes a filling, that self-giving is met by a return gift that far surpasses what was given.

We are celebrating this wedding in the season of Lent. During the forty days of Lent, Christians have traditionally meditated on the isolation, betrayal, passion, and death of Jesus. The liturgical colors of Lent are subdued, and fasting is the rule. This somber season might seem an inappropriate setting for a wedding, but in fact it is not. Marital love is all about imitating Christ in His self-giving, the very act that we remember during Lent. Marital love is about the daily practice of Lent—not the practice of self-affliction and fasting, but the practice of self-giving love. More importantly, Lent is a good time for a wedding because Lent is never the end of the story; it is always, every year, followed by Easter—the greatest example of an event that cannot be adequately explained by what went before, the Event of events, the Surprise of surprises.

Josh and Abby, I urge you both to devote yourselves to practicing Lent throughout your marriage—that is, to devote yourselves to mutual self-giving. And when you do, you can expect the Easter sun to rise again and again. The surprise of love which has overtaken you will be followed by the surprise of love returned. You are embarking on a voyage of self-sacrifice and self-giving. You cannot know where that voyage will lead; you cannot know the depths of self-sacrifice that may be required of you. But you can embark in faith, confident in God's promise that every embarking becomes a journey home, that everyone who gives his life gains his life, that every Lent is followed by Easter, and that for every death, God, the Ever-Living and Eternally Loving God, promises the surprise of resurrection.

In the Name of the Father, and of the Son, and of the Holy Spirit. Amen.

8 MARRIAGE IS DYING

Marriage of Jonathan and Hannah Griffith
August 15, 2003

SCRIPTURE READING

Genesis 2:18–25

Then the LORD God said, "It is not good for the man to be alone; I will make him a helper suitable for him." Out of the ground the LORD God formed every beast of the field and every bird of the sky, and brought them to the man to see what he would call them; and whatever the man called a living creature, that was its name. And the man gave names to all the cattle, and to the birds of the heavens, and to every beast of the field, but for Adam there was not found a helper suitable for him. So the LORD God caused a deep sleep to fall upon the man, and he slept; then He took one of his ribs, and closed up the flesh at that place. And the LORD God built into a woman the rib which He had taken from the man, and brought her to the man. And the man said,

> "This is now bone of my bones,
> And flesh of my flesh.
> She shall be called Woman,
> Because she was taken out of Man."

For this cause a man shall leave his father and his mother, and shall cleave to his wife; and they shall become one flesh. And the man and his wife were both naked, and were not ashamed.

HOMILY

Marriage is dying.[1] That has been a recurrent theme of cultural conservatives for several decades, and statistics support this conclusion. In 2000, 5.4 million couples in the US were living together without marriage. Nearly one-third of American children are being raised without two parents. Some observers have gone further, declaring what amounts to a post-mortem for marriage. Several years ago, Maggie Gallagher published a book called *The Abolition of Marriage*, and more recently the *Weekly Standard* announced the "end of marriage" after the Vermont Supreme Court decided to extend marital rights to homosexual couples.

A number of factors have conspired to produce this crisis: changes in divorce law, cultural shifts during the 1960s and 1970s, the collapse of public morals. Instead of being viewed as a lifetime commitment sealed with an oath before God, marriage has come to be viewed as a temporary alliance that either party can leave without fault. Earlier, a Christian view of marriage was not only instinctively practiced, but also was supported by American institutions. In 1885, the U.S. Supreme Court stated that nothing was more important than that the law give support to "the idea of the family, as consisting in and springing from the union for life of one man and one woman in the holy estate of matrimony." Recently, the Supreme Court issued a decision that encourages a basic redefinition of marriage.

All these are factors, but something more fundamental has happened: Marriage is dying because we have forgotten that marriage is always about dying. The fact that marriage demands death is clear in the first marriage, recorded in Genesis 2. After the Lord had brought all sorts of animals to Adam to see what he would name them, nothing was found suitable for him. So the Lord caused Adam to fall into

---

[1] The substance of this sermon was published as "Why Marriage Is Dying" in *Touchstone*.

a "deep sleep," which describes a state near death, a type and picture of death. And while in that condition of living death, the Lord took out a rib and built a woman for Adam. Adam could rely on God to bring animals to him. But if he was going to have a suitable helper, he would first have to go through "deep sleep." It was not good for him to be alone, but the only way to overcome his solitude was to be split in two. If he was going to have a bride, he would first have to die.

The connection between marriage and death continues into the following chapter of Genesis. When the serpent came to tempt Eve, Adam was not off on the other side of Eden. He was right there beside her the whole time (3:6) and allowed Eve to be tempted and to eat from the tree. Standing beside Eve, Adam was faced with a stark choice: Either Adam would die for his bride, or he would kill her and his marriage. Either he would put himself between the bride and the beast, or he would stand back and leave Eve to be attacked. After the Lord came to confront Adam, he was again faced with this choice: Either he would intercede for his wife, or he would blame her. We know what he did. Adam's sin was his refusal to fight and die for his bride.

What does this all mean for you, Jonathan and Hannah, today? For you as for Adam, dying begins at this wedding. On his wedding day, Adam went through the "deep sleep" of death in order to receive a wife. And this wedding is also a ceremony of dying. Jonathan and Hannah, you have spent the better part of your lives under the oversight of your parents. They have provided physical necessities, loved and cared for you, instructed you, and set an example for you in ways that no one can fully understand. Today, that world dies. And when that world dies, you die too. This wedding marks the end of that Jonathan and that Hannah, the end of your old world, of your old securities.

The wedding is only the beginning of death. If you go through this ceremony and then continue to live as you have always lived, you have not understood the first thing about this ceremony. Jonathan, if you continue the habits of a single man, you are mocking the marriage vows you take today. Jonathan, if you do not give your life to guard and support and nourish your wife, you are not keeping your vows, and God will hold you accountable. Hannah, if you live as if you were unmarried, you are not fulfilling your calling. Hannah, if you do not give your life to help and support your husband, you are not keeping your vows, and God will hold you accountable.

Nearly four decades ago, Alexander Schmemann said that the problem with modern marriage "is not adultery or lack of 'adjustment' or 'mental cruelty.'" Instead, the problem is the "idolization of the family" that identifies "marriage with happiness" and refuses "to accept the cross in it." God's presence as a "third party" in the marriage spells "the death of the marriage as something only 'natural,'" and directs it to its true end of the kingdom of God. In short, Schmemann argued, the glory of marriage is "that of the martyr's crown. For the way to the Kingdom is the *matyria*—bearing witness to Christ. And this means crucifixion and suffering. A marriage that does not constantly crucify its own selfishness and self-sufficiency, which does not 'die to itself' that it may point beyond itself, is not a Christian marriage."[2]

Though marriage is dying, and marriage requires death, young people continue to get married willingly and joyfully. Jonathan and Hannah, you are here voluntarily to take these oaths. Either you are simply ignorant of what you're doing, or you have some hope that the death involved in marriage does not have the final word. Getting married is either an act of supreme folly, or it is an act of faith. More precisely, it is folly or an act of faith in resurrection, in the

---

[2] These quotations are from *For the Life of the World* (Crestwood, N.Y.: St. Vladimir's Seminary Press, 1963), chap. 5.

certainty of new life; it is hope that a new and better life lies on the other side of this death. At this point, we see that our secular world is profoundly ill-equipped to support marriage. Secularism promises that marriage will be a means of self-realization, and couples are astonished to find that it demands continual self-denial. Secularism sends the newlyweds off in a shower of birdseed, without warning them that together with the happiness of marriage they will face heartache and the thousand natural shocks that flesh is heir to. Secularism sends them unsuspectingly to death and refuses to offer any hope of resurrection.

You, by contrast, come willingly to die at the wedding, because you believe the gospel that announces Jesus is risen indeed. Because He is raised from the dead, we hope that we too will one day be raised, and we also hope that all the little dyings that we experience in life will lead to resurrections. You can welcome the death that marriage brings because you follow a master who said, "Whoever wishes to save his life shall lose it; but whoever loses his life for My sake will find it" (Matt. 16:25), and "unless a grain of wheat falls into the earth and dies, it remains alone; but if it dies, it bears much fruit" (Jn. 12:24).

I began with reference to the "death of Adam" in the garden, the death necessary for him to obtain a bride. Adam is the great example of a bad husband because he didn't learn the lesson of his wedding day, the lesson that marriage demands death. But Scripture also gives us a portrait of the perfect Husband, Jesus. On the cross, the Last Adam went to actual death, a real "deep sleep," for the sake of His bride. On the cross, Jesus' side was opened so that water and blood could pour out for the cleansing and refreshment of His bride. On the cross, Jesus the Good Shepherd laid down His life for His sheep, and Jesus the faithful Husband laid down His life for His bride. All that Adam failed to do, Jesus did, and in doing this, Jesus transformed a bride who had become a whore into a beautiful bride, spotless and without wrinkle or blemish. He did all this, Scripture tells us, for the "joy set before Him" (Heb. 12:2), for the joy of resurrection, for the joy of consummation with His bride, in the hope of resurrection.

Jonathan and Hannah, your marriage will live only if from this day forward you devote yourselves to continual dying, only if you die daily in hope of resurrection life.

In the Name of the Father, and of the Son, and of the Holy Spirit. Amen.

9 GOD BUILT A WOMAN

Marriage of Otto and Bethany Nielson
October 2, 2004

SCRIPTURE READING

Genesis 2:21–23

So the LORD God caused a deep sleep to fall upon the man, and he slept; then He took one of his ribs, and closed up the flesh at that place. And the LORD God fashioned into a woman the rib which He had taken from the man, and brought her to the man. And the man said,

"This is now bone of my bones;
And flesh of my flesh;
She shall be called Woman,
Because she was taken out of Man."

OPENING PRAYER

Almighty God, our heavenly Father, You gave a bride to Adam, and You sent Your Son to rescue His bride. Send now Your Spirit to lighten the darkness of our hearts, so the words of our mouths and the meditations of our hearts may be acceptable in Your sight, O Lord, our Strength and our Redeemer. Amen.

HOMILY

I have just read that the Lord God fashioned Adam's rib into a woman, but that is not precisely what the original

Hebrew says. The Hebrew says that the Lord God took a rib and "built" a woman for Adam.

That's an odd way to talk about making a woman, but the oddity is a significant one because it points to one of the key differences between the first Adam and the last. Yahweh formed the first Adam from the dust and placed him in a garden that Yahweh Himself had planted. Then, the Lord built a wife and brought her to the man. With the Last Adam, the situation is reversed. The Last Adam (like Noah after the Flood) plants His own garden. And quite unlike the first Adam, the Last Adam does not receive a bride built by His Father. On the contrary, the Last Adam builds His own bride, and having built her He protects her from Satanic assault: "Upon this rock I will build My church," Jesus says, "And the gates of Hades will not overcome it" (Matt. 16:18).

Otto, it may seem that your situation is closer to Adam's than to Jesus'. After all, you didn't *create* Bethany; you were not around when she was born, and you had nothing to do with building her character. The foundations of her life were laid at home by her parents, at school by her teachers, and through experiences she had before she ever imagined that she might fall for a guy named Otto. This is an essential perspective on your marriage. You were in deep sleep, and the Lord built Bethany and brought her to you. Bethany is a gift of God, undeserved as any other gift, and your first and last and lifelong response to this gift must be gratitude—gratitude like the ecstasy of Adam when he awoke to find his bride: "This is now bone of my bones, flesh of my flesh; she shall be called Woman, because she was taken out of Man."

As true and essential as that perspective is, it is also true that you are called to be like the Last Adam. Paul is quite explicit about that. In Ephesians 5, he quotes from Genesis 2 ("for this cause a man shall leave his father and his mother and cleave to his wife, and the two shall be one flesh") but he immediately reminds his readers that he is not talking about the first Adam: "I speak about Christ and the church." Otto, you are called to be a husband like the Last Adam, and that means you are called to be the kind of husband who builds his own bride.

What can this possibly mean? It hardly seems reasonable or fair that you have been given this God-like task of building a woman. It is a God-like task, but it is not mystical or bizarre. The New Testament term for what you are called to do is "edify," which simply means "build." God has built a wife for you, and you are called to build her up, adorning her so she is translated from glory to more radiant glory, from beauty to more perfect beauty, from joy to deeper joy.

In the same letter where Paul instructs Christian men to love their wives as Christ loves the church, he also gives some instruction about edification, a blueprint for building the bride of Christ, which is also a plan for building up a wife (Eph. 4:25–32). Paul says to "lay aside falsehood" and "speak truth." He says, "Be angry, and yet do not sin; do not let the sun go down on your anger, and do not give the devil an opportunity." He says, "Let no rotten word proceed from your mouth, but only such a word as is good for edification according to the need of the moment, that it may give grace to those who hear." He says, "Do not grieve the Holy Spirit," and "let all bitterness and wrath and anger and clamor and slander be put away from you, along with all malice." He says, "Be kind to one another, tender-hearted, forgiving each other, just as God in Christ also has forgiven you." The Lord ripped a rib from the first Adam to build a bride; Jesus voluntarily gave His entire body on the cross so that His bride could be born from the water and blood that flowed from His side. That is how you, Otto, are to edify, to build up, your wife—by giving your life for her sake.

To learn that a husband is called to build his wife is alarming. Even more alarming is the fact that the bride participates in the building project. In this respect, the last Eve transcends the first Eve as completely as Jesus surpasses Adam. Jesus builds His church so that He can present her to Himself glorious, without spot or wrinkle. Yet each member is also called to edify—to build up—the church. Jesus builds His bride, and as He does, the bride builds herself. And yet more: In building herself, the bride is also building Christ, who *is* the one body with many members. The church is "being built into a spiritual house," but that divine passive envelops and drives human activity that "builds up the body of Christ," the body that is the bride. Christ builds the bride so that the bride builds herself, which in turn builds Christ. Mary is the model here for all Christians: God sovereignly formed Mary to be the new Eve, but Mary said, "Behold, the bondslave of the Lord; may it be done to me according to your word" (Lk. 1:38). And so, Mary became a participant in forming Christ, as Christ took form in her. "He who loves his own wife loves himself," Paul says (Eph. 5:28), and he who edifies his wife builds up himself.

Bethany, this means that you are not merely the passive object of a construction project. Otto is called to build you, to edify you, to lay himself down, in Christ, as a cornerstone for your life. But you, in response, are to build him, and in the same way that Paul outlines: Speak words that build, not words that destroy; don't allow the sun to go down on your anger; be tender-hearted, forgiving each other, as God in Christ has forgiven you.

To capture the complex beauty of this picture, the metaphor of building eventually becomes unwieldy. We are not accustomed to buildings that build themselves, much less buildings that turn around and somehow build their builder. We need something more supple to capture the whole biblical truth, and when we need something more supple we turn, naturally, to music. Christ and His bride are fugally related: Christ the Head is the theme, but the bride follows as a melody of her own, which keeps in step with the melody of her husband. Christ's song blazes the path for the song of the bride and provides the aural space in which the bride's song is sung; the bride's song is always to harmonize with Christ's and never to drown out His voice. But, responsive and secondary though it is, the song of the bride also builds up and adorns the song of her husband. The duet is miraculously richer than the solo. This is a great mystery, but I speak of Christ and the church.

So too, marriage is harmonics, the lifelong fugal dance in which the husband's song calls for the bride, and the bride's song adorns her husband's, so that they are together a single song. Marriage is designed to be truly a Song of Songs.

None of this is within the range of human possibility. We are not capable of building another human being. In our sin and folly, we are instead like the foolish woman who tears down her house with her own hands. Nor are we capable of the kind of harmonizing required for two lives to become a single song, for discord rather than harmony is the fundamental condition of sinful human existence. Marital harmony is not within human possibility, but it is possible. It is possible by the power of the Spirit who proceeds from the Father and the Son, the Spirit who gives us the freedom to become and to be what we, in ourselves, could never become or be.

Otto and Bethany, this is our prayer for you on your wedding day: that you may build one another in the power of the Spirit, and that your lives may harmonize as you both harmonize on the melody of the Spirit, the melody that is the Spirit. May the Spirit of Christ fill your home—the Spirit who hovered over the waters and formed the earth into a dwelling place for God; the Spirit who gave wisdom to Bezalel and Oholiab to build the tabernacle, and the Spirit who gave Solomon wisdom for the temple; the Spirit who hovered over the womb of Mary to shape a new creation, and the Spirit that flowed from Jesus as living water for a living bride; the Spirit poured out at Pentecost to build the church, and the Spirit who equips each member to share in that construction; the Spirit who is, with the Son, the Divine Architect and the Divine Builder; the Spirit who is the Eternal Musician, whose movement is the eternal rhythm of triune life, who is the Eternal Music of the Eternal God.

Closing Prayer

Almighty God, our Father, who made all things at the beginning through Your Spirit and Your Son, give grace to Otto and Bethany, that they might build up one another in faithful love to their life's end, so that You may be pleased with the song of praise that their life becomes. Through Jesus Christ our Lord, who lives and reigns with You and with the Spirit, ever one God, unto ages of ages. Amen.

10 IT TAKES A CHURCH

Marriage of Andrew and Anneke Stafford
August 20, 2004

SCRIPTURE READING

Genesis 2:22–24

The LORD God fashioned into a woman the rib which He had taken from the man. . . .

For this reason a man shall leave his father and his mother, and be joined to his wife; and they shall become one flesh.

Ephesians 4:1–3; 5:24–25

I therefore, the prisoner of the Lord, entreat you to walk in a manner worthy of the calling with which you have been called, with all humility and gentleness, with patience, showing forbearance to each other in love, being diligent to preserve the unity of the Spirit in the bond of peace. . . .

But as the church is subject to Christ, so also the wives ought to be to their husbands in everything. Husbands, love your wives, just as Christ also loved the church and gave Himself up for her.

OPENING PRAYER

Almighty God, our Father, give us grace to hear and understand Your word, and to live faithfully before You, so that we may be pleasing to You. For the sake of Jesus Christ, Your Son, our Lord, who lives and reigns with You and with the Holy Spirit, ever one God, unto ages of ages. Amen.

HOMILY

Andrew and Anneke, you know what the Lord requires of you in your marriage. You have heard the teachings of Genesis and Ephesians today, and you have heard them often before. You have listened repeatedly as the biblical teaching on marriage has been explained at length, and you have observed Christian families living together. You know that in your marriage you are called to humility, gentleness, patience, forbearance, and love. You are being knit together today in and by the Spirit, the Divine Matchmaker, and you know that you must be diligent to preserve this unity of the Spirit in the bond of peace. That is how you walk worthy of the calling to which you have been called.

Of course, from this day on, you will begin to know these things in a way that you haven't known them before. There's a kind of knowledge that comes only in doing—in marriage as in so many other areas of life. You are about to begin the doing. And, from this day on, you will be practicing and working out these things in specific ways and circumstances. Andrew, you are promising to love and cherish Anneke, not some "woman in general." Anneke, you are taking an oath to love and respect Andrew, not some capital-M "Man." You will be living as husband and wife in specific circumstances, which may involve unforeseen wealth or poverty, success or failure, sickness or health, or some rewarding combination of all of these. There is no generic marriage—only *this* man and *this* woman made one flesh.

But to ensure that your marriage will flourish, it is not enough to know positively what marriage should be. Adam knew he was one flesh with his wife, but he was unprepared for the serpent's assault on his bride. So too, it is important to understand the kinds of threats you will face, threats that conspire to make you forget what you know, or, failing that, to seduce you from doing what you know to be right. In Eden, Satan took the form of a talking serpent; you need to know what forms he is likely to take when he comes to threaten your Eden.

We live in an age of sexual liberation, and this liberation is basically an attempt to break the constraints that marriage, family, and community place on sexual life. By the terms of this liberation, every desire is equal to every other, and the boundaries of tolerable sexual and marital behavior have expanded dramatically. As Wendell Berry has said,[1] "Divorce on an epidemic scale is all right; child abandonment by one parent or another is all right . . . promiscuity is all right; adultery is all right. Promiscuity among teenagers is pretty much all right, for 'that's the way it is'; abortion as birth control is all right; the prostitution of sex in advertisements and public entertainment is all right." Only at the distant margins does our culture attempt to set up a few arbitrary limits on sexual freedom: child molestation (particularly by priests), sexual violence, sexual harassment, unwanted pregnancy, and venereal diseases—these are not all right. But, the efforts to leash in sexual liberation are futile: "Trying to draw the line where we are trying to draw it," Berry writes, "between carelessness and brutality, is like insisting that falling is flying—until you hit the ground—and then trying to outlaw hitting the ground."

If sexual liberation were an isolated feature of contemporary life, it would not be too difficult to resist. We could all be like Joseph, flee youthful lusts, and be done with it. But sexual liberation is part of a much larger pattern that involves the deterioration of communities. Sexual liberation

---

[1] All quotations from Berry are taken from the title essay of *Sex, Economy, Freedom, and Community: Eight Essays* (New York: Knopf, 1994). The entire homily, in various ways, is indebted to the essay.

destroys communities because it destroys trust. All the advertisements, movies, TV shows, books, and magazines that encourage sexual freedom constitute a complex assault, and in some cases a conscious assault, not only on marital faithfulness but also on community trust. How can you befriend your neighbor when he might be hitting on your wife?

But the impact goes in the other direction as well. Fragmented and weak communities weaken marriages, and in ways obvious and subtle our world is at war with community, or, to be concrete, the world is at war with the communion that is the Christian church. As you both well know, the attacks on the church take intellectual form in heresy and militant atheism. But the subtle threats are equally dangerous and are deeply engraved in the physical arrangements, patterns, and structures of our lives. How can a church be a vibrant community when the members live an hour away from each other and from the church, when the members see each other for only an hour a week? What kind of community can develop when you never pass your neighbors on the sidewalk, but only on the street, when you are both comfortably encased in a soundproof, air-conditioned bubble of glass and steel? How much help will friends be to your marriage if you are able to squeeze out time to speak to them only a few times a year, on the handful of evenings you are not working late at the office?

So there is a vicious circle: Modern life weakens the church, which undermines marriages, which in turn further undermines the church. This means that whatever threatens the trust, forbearance, unity, peace, compassion, forgiveness, and love of a Christian community threatens your marriage too. Your vigilance to preserve your marriage must extend beyond the walls of your own home. If you want your marriage to flourish, you must be diligent not only to maintain unity with each other, but also to keep the unity of the Spirit in the bond of peace with other believers, and make conscious choices to ensure that this is practically possible. It is not enough to be ready when the serpent comes knocking at the door, because he has the capability to launch his darts from long range.

So there is also a benevolent circle: In a healthy Christian community, a family is never alone, but woven into a larger network of trust, mutual help, and loving sacrifice. In a healthy community, friends, neighbors, fellow church members, and extended families all assist in helping a married couple stay faithful to their marriage vows. And healthy marriages, in turn, strengthen the church. Marriage joins a man and woman to each other and also binds them to the wider community, both past and future. Marriage is the intersection where past generations of your separate families cross and mingle, and marriage joins you to the generations to come. And so, healthy churches help marriages flourish, and flourishing marriages make for healthy churches.

This benevolent circle does not come about without effort. It never has. Already in the first century, the Ephesians had to be diligent to preserve the unity and peace of the church, and you must be no less diligent. This is the conclusion of the matter: Cultivate the unity and peace of your marriage for the sake of the Christian community, and cultivate the unity and peace of the church for the sake of your marriage. And do all this with your whole heart, to the glory of God, the Father of your Lord, Jesus Christ.

In the Name of the Father, and of the Son, and of the Holy Spirit. Amen.

11 LOVE MADE FOOD

Marriage of Joel and Jordan Myers
July 16, 2004

SCRIPTURE READING

Proverbs 9:1–6, 13–18

Wisdom has built her house,
She has hewn out her seven pillars;
She has prepared her food, she has mixed her wine;
She has also set her table;
She has sent out her maidens, she calls
From the tops of the heights of the city:
"Whoever is naïve, let him turn in here!"
To him who lacks understanding she says,
"Come, eat of my food
And drink of the wine I have mixed.
Forsake your folly and live,
And proceed in the way of understanding." . . .

The woman of folly is boisterous;
She is naïve and knows nothing.
And she sits by the doorway of her house,
On a seat by the high places of the city,
Calling to those who pass by,
Who are making their paths straight:
"Whoever is naïve, let him turn in here,"
And to him to lacks understanding she says,
"Stolen water is sweet;
And bread eaten in secret is pleasant."

But he does not know that the dead are there,
That her guests are in the depths of Sheol.

OPENING PRAYER

Almighty God, our Father, we give You thanks that You have offered us a place at the banquet of Wisdom. Fill us with Your Spirit of Wisdom and Grace, the Spirit of Jesus Christ, who is the Wisdom of God, so that we may eat and drink only from Wisdom's table; do all this through Jesus Christ our Lord. Amen.

HOMILY

"Look how far we've come." "It's been a long, bumpy road." "We can't turn back now." "We're at a crossroads." "We may have to go our separate ways." "The relationship isn't going anywhere." "We're spinning our wheels." "Our relationship is off the track." "The marriage is on the rocks." "We may have to bail out of this relationship."

All these expressions and many more like them assume a popular picture of love and marriage—love is a journey. The metaphor has been further elaborated: "The lovers are travelers on a journey together, with their common life goals seen as destinations to be reached. The relationship is their vehicle, and it allows them to pursue those common goals together. The relationship is seen as fulfilling its purpose as long as it allows them to make progress toward their common goals. The journey isn't easy. There are impediments, and there are places (crossroads) where a decision has to be made about which direction to go in and whether to keep traveling together."[1]

---

[1] The quotations in these two paragraphs are taken from a summary discussion of George Lakoff and Mark Johnson's book *Metaphors We Live By* (Chicago: University of Chicago Press, 1980), available at <http://www.ac.wwu.edu/~market/semiotic/met1.html>. The following paragraphs are also inspired by the work of Lakoff and Johnson.

Metaphors such as "Love is a journey" are often dismissed as unnecessary window dressing. When we want to communicate clearly, we speak literally. But when we want to write poetry, compose a speech, or prepare a wedding sermon, we grasp for analogies, images, and metaphors. Metaphor is sauce to tasteless food; it adds flavor, but the food is food regardless. But that view is completely wrong. Our language is shot through with metaphor, even when—especially when—we think we are speaking literally. Metaphor is an irreducible element in our speech.

And this is not only the case in our language; metaphors and images are irreducible elements in our thoughts, plans, and actions. Metaphors motivate us and shape our lives. Images provoke and discipline our desires because they fuel and energize imagination. When we say, "Love is a journey," we are not merely connecting two realms of life. We are identifying certain important features of love: love takes time, love develops and moves, love seeks certain ends or goals. This metaphor tells us what to expect in marriage—that not every road is equally smooth, that at times we will have to slog uphill and at other times we can coast, and that some marriages run out of gas or crash and burn before reaching their destination.

Joel and Jordan, as you enter into a marriage covenant today, it is worth pondering this question: What metaphors and images should shape your expectations, hopes, dreams, and actions in marriage?

According to Scripture, marriage is fundamentally metaphorical. The very essence of marriage is to be a picture of something else: the union of Jesus Christ and His church. There are many other images of marriage in Scripture as well, but this evening we'll examine only one of these. Proverbs 9 uses one of the most common biblical metaphors for love and marriage—the image of the banquet, the analogy of food. This is not the first time Solomon uses this metaphor in Proverbs. Throughout the first eight chapters,

Solomon teaches his son about two women, Lady Wisdom and Lady Folly, both of whom seek the attention of the young prince. And throughout these chapters, Solomon frequently describes sex in terms of food, equates hunger with sexual desire, and renders an invitation to bed as an invitation to a table. Warning against the adulterous woman, he tells his son, "Drink water from your own cistern, and fresh water from your own well" (Prov. 5:15). In Proverbs 7, the seductress entices the foolish young man with promises of spices and drink: "I have sprinkled my bed with myrrh, aloes, and cinnamon. Come, let us drink our fill of love until morning; let us delight ourselves with caresses" (7:17–18). The young man goes off like an "ox to the slaughter" (7:22), and in her house of death the seductress devours him.

There are more positive uses of this metaphor as well. "Your love is better than wine," says the bride of the Song of Songs (1:2), and later she describes her lover as an apple tree loaded with fruit (2:3, 5). And the man responds in kind: "Your lips, my bride, drip honey; honey and milk are under your tongue" (4:11), and he speaks of his bride as a garden full of "choice fruits" for her husband to taste and "eat" (4:13, 16).

But how is marriage, how is love, like a banquet? What kind of life does this metaphor imply? What does this metaphor teach us about marriage?

In Scripture the deep connection between food and marital love is the covenant. A covenant is a lifelong union between two persons. In marriage, this union is symbolized in many ways; for example, by the fact that husband and wife share a common name. Jordan came here today as Jordan Amos, but she will leave as Jordan Myers. That union is symbolized in Scripture with a common robe: "Spread your covering over your maid," Ruth says to Boaz on the threshing floor (Ruth 3:9). That union is symbolized in the physical act of sex, uniting a man and woman quite unmetaphorically as one flesh. Food is also a symbol of union. In the Old Testament, there was an animal slaughtered for sacrifice, and when the worshipers all ate from it, they became one. In the New Testament, there is one loaf of bread, and we are all one body because we partake of the one loaf. Food, like marriage, binds two into one flesh and by one flesh. If marriage is a banquet, that means that you, Joel and Jordan, have become one flesh; you partake of a common table, a common plate, a common cup, and you are called to pursue an increasingly intimate union.

For humans at least, food is never simply for sustenance, never merely fuel for a biological machine. Food is also for delight; it brings pleasure. Scripture celebrates the abundance and variety of food that God has created. God offers every fruit-bearing tree to Adam and Eve, and He promises figs, grapes, pomegranates, and raisins to Israel. The Lord gives Israel a land flowing with milk and honey, and He requires that every sacrifice be seasoned with salt. At the temple, Israel feasts on beef, mutton, lamb, and varieties of bread, all washed down with strong drink. Joel and Jordan, since your marriage is a meal, you are called to take delight in one another, and to give delight to one another; you are called to taste and celebrate your distinct flavors, and you must never lose your taste for one another.

In Scripture, there are clean and unclean meats, foods permitted and forbidden. For Israel, unclean animals symbolized idolatrous nations, and avoiding unclean food reinforced Israel's separateness and her exclusive devotion to Yahweh. Solomon makes the same point with his story of Lady Wisdom and Lady Folly. Both offer food, and choosing Wisdom's table means renouncing the table of Folly. Joel and Jordan, by the vows you take today, you are declaring that you have chosen to feast only on each other, and that means every other table, every other banquet, is off limits. You are committing to sit at the same table together until death, and so you must resist any enticements to share in another feast. Here there is a difference between marriage and a banquet: Banquets are public and communal, while the feast of marriage is private and intimate. It is a table reserved for two.

Finally, at a banquet, food is shared. Only barbarians gorge themselves without concern for anyone else; civilized people restrain themselves and leave food on the tray for others. Bread is broken and passed from hand to hand, forming a circle of table "companions." In the banquet of marriage, you are to share selflessly all that you are and all that you have. Your gifts and talents, your time and energies, your wealth and goods are food, which each of you freely puts at the other's disposal. Joel, strive to turn everything the Lord places in your hands into food to nourish and sustain and give pleasure to Jordan; and Jordan, do the same. Feast on one another, and be diligent to prepare a continual feast for one another.

Today you begin the banquet of your marriage. May your marriage be full of variety and spice and surprise. Above all, strive to make your marriage banquet a banquet of wisdom, a marriage banquet founded on the true wisdom that comes from the fear of God. And, as the Lord blesses, may your table be like the table of Psalm 128: "Your wife shall be like a fruitful vine within your house, your children like olive plants around your table. Behold, for thus shall the man be blessed who fears the LORD" (vv. 3–4).

In the Name of the Father, and of the Son, and of the Holy Spirit. Amen.

12 THE BETTER WINE

Marriage of Woelke and Megan Leithart
May 18, 2004

SCRIPTURE READING

Song of Songs 1:1–7
The Song of Songs, which is Solomon's.
"May he kiss me with the kisses of his mouth!
For your love is better than wine.
Your oils have a pleasing fragrance,
Your name is like purified oil;
Therefore the maidens love you.
Draw me after you and let us run together!
The king has brought me into his chambers."
"We will rejoice in you and be glad;
We will extol your love more than wine.
Rightly do they love you."
"I am black but lovely,
O daughters of Jerusalem,
Like the tents of Kedar,
like the curtains of Solomon.
Do not stare at me because I am swarthy,
For the sun has burned me.
My mother's sons were angry with me;
They made me caretaker of the vineyards,
But I have not taken care of my own vineyard.
Tell me, O you whom my soul loves,
Where do you pasture your flock,
Where do you make it lie down at noon?

For why should I be like one who veils herself
Beside the flocks of your companions?"

Homily

"May he kiss me with the kisses of his mouth! For your
love is better than wine." So says the bride at the beginning
of the Song of Songs, and the chorus agrees: "We will rejoice in you and be glad; we will extol your love more than
wine" (1:4). Later the bridegroom responds in kind: "How
beautiful is your love, my sister, my bride! How much better is your love than wine" (4:10) and "I have come into my
garden, my sister, my bride; I have gathered my myrrh along
with my balsam, I have eaten my honeycomb and my honey;
I have drunk my wine and my milk. Eat, friends; drink and
imbibe deeply, O lovers" (5:1). The bridegroom describes
his bride's navel as a "round goblet which never lacks mixed
wine" (7:2), and her mouth is "like the best wine" (7:9).
The bride longs to lead her lover into a house, where she
"would give her lover spiced wine to drink from the juice
of her pomegranates" (8:2). The Song of Songs is not the
only place where Solomon compares love to wine. In Proverbs, he urges his son to "rejoice in the wife of your youth"
and be "intoxicated always with her love" (Prov. 5:18–19).

For the bridegroom in the Song of Songs, the bride's
body is a vineyard, a garden, a field, a promised land flowing with milk and honey, where the bridegroom can gather
fruits for the intoxicating wine of love. "A garden locked
is my sister, my bride," says the bridegroom, "a rock garden locked, a spring sealed up" (Song 4:12). She is a garden of pomegranates, of spices and aloes, a garden spring
that runs with fresh water. In response, the bride unlocks
the gate of her garden to her lover: "May my beloved come
into his garden and eat its choice fruits" (4:16). Every bridegroom who rejoices that he is one flesh with his bride is a
new Adam; every bride who is a garden of delights for her

husband is a new Eve; every godly and loving marriage, however marred by sin, is a reestablishment of Eden.

Yahweh too has a vineyard, and this vineyard is His bride. According to Isaiah 5, the Lord planted a vineyard on a fertile hill, "dug it all around, removed its stones, and planted it with the choicest vine. And He built a tower in the middle of it, and hewed out a wine vat in it" (v. 2). He put a hedge around her, and built a wall for her protection. Yahweh established His bride, His vineyard, and expected to gather good fruit from her, to make wine that gladdens the heart of man and the heart of God.

Yahweh has a garden and a bride, a garden that is His bride; and Adam, His image, was given a bride and a garden, a bride that was his garden. These come together in Jesus, who is both Last Adam and Yahweh in flesh, who comes into the world as a bridegroom, a lover, and a caretaker of a vineyard. As the bridegroom, Jesus comes not only with the wine of love but with the wine of joy. When John the Baptist announces the coming of Jesus, he says, "He who has the bride is the bridegroom; but the friend of the bridegroom, who stands and hears him, rejoices greatly because of the bridegroom's voice. And so this joy of mine has been made full" (Jn. 3:29).

Even before Jesus is explicitly identified as the bridegroom in John's gospel, He fulfills the role of bridegroom at the wedding of Cana, where He turned water to wine (Jn. 2:1–11). It was customary in that day for the bridegroom to provide the wine for a wedding feast, so by providing wine, Jesus has taken over the responsibility of the bridegroom. Jesus' role as the bridegroom overarches the entire gospel of John and the book of Revelation.[1] He is identified as the bridegroom at the beginning of the gospel, and the

---

[1] These comments are indebted to the work of Warren Gage, some of which is available at <http://www.knoxseminary.org/Prospective/Faculty/FacultyForum/JohnRevelationProject/index.html>.

bride is revealed at the end of Revelation. At the beginning of John's gospel, the Spirit descends from heaven to anoint Jesus; at the end of Revelation, the bride descends from heaven to be joined to her husband. The entirety of John's two-volume work is about the revelation of Jesus the bridegroom and the coming of the bride.

Dotted throughout John's romance are other references to the fullness of joy that the bridegroom brings. Jesus describes Himself as the vine at the center of an Edenic garden, and He speaks as the true bridegroom, the Last Adam, instructing His disciples to keep His commandments so that they can abide in His love. He gives these instructions, He says, so "that My joy may be in you, and that your joy may be made full." Jesus further encourages His disciples, "Ask and you will receive, that your joy may be made full." As Jesus goes to the Father, He tells the Father that He has spoken the Father's words in the world, so that His own joy might be made full in His bride. Throughout John's writings, Jesus is the bridegroom who provides the wine of joy.

Woelke, today you are taking Megan not only as your bride but also as your garden, your vineyard, and you are called to tend her, to beautify her, to set a wall of protection around her. Bring joy to your bride, as Jesus does to His, by your presence with her, by your words, by giving her what she needs and asks, by your comfort and encouragement in the midst of inevitable sorrows and challenges. Be intoxicated always with her love. Megan, today you admit this man and this man alone into your garden. May you find his love better than wine, and may you be filled with the wine of joy. You are called to bear fruit for the joy and delight of your husband—the fruit of beauty, of order, of grace, of peace, of comfort—the fruit, under the Lord's blessing, of children.

One of the most striking things that Jesus does as bridegroom is to save the better wine for later. At the wedding in Cana, the headwaiter is astonished at this departure from custom, and the astonishment for ancient readers would have gone much deeper. Ancient man was convinced that the later was always worse, the supplement always a degeneration from the origin. But Jesus reversed that. Though ancient man believed that the golden age was past, perhaps never to be recovered, Jesus proclaimed the *future* coming of God's kingdom. Though ancient man believed that a woman was a defective man, Scripture teaches that the woman, who comes second, is the glory of the man. Where ancient man served the best wine first, Jesus serves the better at the end of the feast. This later wine is the fullness of love and the fullness of joy.

This is wonderfully captured in one of the most beautiful passages of Alexander Schmemann's beautiful book, *For the Life of the World*: "In movies and magazines," he writes, "the 'icon' of marriage is always a youthful couple. But once, in the light and warmth of an autumn afternoon, I saw on the bench of a public square, in a poor Parisian suburb, an old and poor couple. They were sitting hand in hand, in silence, enjoying the pale light, the last warmth of the season. In silence: all words had been said, all passion exhausted, all storms at peace. The whole life was behind— yet all of it was now *present*, in this silence, in this light, in this warmth, in this silent unity of hands. Present—and ready for eternity, ripe for joy. This to me remains the vision of marriage, of its heavenly beauty."[2] Of course, there is a vision of heavenly beauty also in the passions of youth. But, Woelke and Megan, don't forget that the better wine comes later. As joyful as you are today, as joyful as your family and friends are today, this is, by comparison with what is to come, only the water of your marriage. By the power of the Bridegroom, it will be transfigured into wine— into fine, aged wine.

---

[2] *For the Life of the World* (Crestwood, N.Y.: St. Vladimir's Seminary Press, 1963), 90.

But—and this is absolutely essential—you cannot expect to enjoy the wine of love or the wine of joy unless you have also received another intoxicant, the Spirit of Jesus. And the Spirit's effect is like the effect of wine: when the Jews saw how the apostles were acting at Pentecost, they believed that they were drunk with new wine, and Paul exhorted the Ephesians not to be drunk with wine but to be filled— "inebriated," St. Ambrose said—with the Spirit. Pentecost is less than two weeks away, and let that be a marker for your marriage—pray that your entire marriage will be carried out under the rubric of Pentecost. Walking in the Spirit will bring a harvest of love and joy, and nothing else will.

And so, Woelke and Megan, cling to one another, but cling also to the Divine Bridegroom. Drink deeply of one another, but even more, drink deeply of the Spirit. Be intoxicated in joyful love and loving joy, but above all, be inebriated by the Spirit. For these three bear witness of heavenly life: the Spirit, the love, and the joy. And these three are one.

In the Name of the Father, and of the Son, and of the Holy Spirit. Amen.

CLOSING PRAYER

Father, You have created all things for our enjoyment, bread to strengthen us and wine to gladden our hearts; fill Woelke and Megan's marriage with the wine of joy. Jesus, our Bridegroom, You have given Yourself in love for Your bride, and shed Your own blood so that we could live; fill Woelke and Megan's marriage with the wine of love. Holy Spirit, You are the Divine Matchmaker, Lord and Giver of all life; fill Woelke and Megan with all grace, and make them fruitful. Father, Son, and Spirit, whose glories in the end will surpass the glories of the beginning, dwell with Woelke and Megan, so that their lives may be transformed from glory to greater glory, from joy to greater joy, from love to greater love, to the glory of Your name. Amen.

13 ARTIFICE AND LOVE

Marriage of Dan and Jessica Klier
November 24, 2001

SCRIPTURE READING

Genesis 2:23
>And the man said,
>"This is now bone of my bones,
>And flesh of my flesh;
>She shall be called Woman,
>Because she was taken out of Man."

HOMILY

Weddings celebrate a beginning. Through a wedding, something is created that didn't exist before. A man and woman are transformed into a husband and wife, two individuals become a couple, two *I*s become a *we*, two are made one flesh. This is not magic, but it is a miracle. God speaks, and behold, all things are made new.

But the truth about a wedding, about a marriage, or about love isn't revealed all at once at the beginning. The ultimate truth of things always comes at the end of things. The full truth about the murder mystery is revealed in the final chapter when the detective unmasks the murderer and reveals that the butler had nothing to do with it. The full disclosure of the symphony's beauty comes with its final chords. The point of a worship service becomes evident when the congregation sits at the Lord's table to eat and drink in the presence of God. The success of our childrearing is evident only when our children become adults. The value of our work is evident only when we've finished the job.

Far from revealing the truth about things, beginnings often obscure reality, and this is nowhere more common than in marriage. How many marriages begin just as this one is beginning—in joy, in beauty, in celebration, only to end in rancor and hatred? How many marriages start with the same air of excitement, the same sense of anticipation, only to end in blank indifference? How many husbands who begin with passion and delight eventually find their wives distasteful, and how many wives who begin with respect come to loathe their husbands?

Marriage and love can be either comic or tragic, and that outcome depends not on how it begins but on how it ends. On the stage, tragedies are always dramatic, ending with flamboyant displays of passion. Real-life tragedies are not so interesting. Real-life tragedies are often perfectly commonplace: another evening with husband and wife peering dully at the TV screen in order to avoid having to look at or talk to one another. That is hardly dramatic, but it is tragic.

I do not wish to put a damper on today's festivities, but marital tragedy is far too common in our day for us to ignore it. We can't pretend that every marriage remains as wonderful as the wedding day. No one starts out marriage hoping for tragedy, and so it's necessary for us to ask how it happens and how it can be avoided. How does love end in tragedy? Why do so many marriages today end in hatred or indifference?

There are some obvious reasons, and many of them boil down to a misunderstanding of love. In our world, love is seen mainly as emotional or sexual. To be in love is to have certain feelings and desires. And if that is the meaning of love, then tragedy is almost inevitable. Feelings can change in a moment, and desires shift from one object to another at the speed of sight. What happens when you lose that loving feeling, when the desire is satisfied, when someone more desirable comes along? Love evaporates; love dies; love ends in tragedy.

But there is a more fundamental reason why such a love is inherently tragic. If love is merely a feeling or desire, then the object of love is no more than a means for indulging that feeling or satisfying that desire. "I love you" comes to mean "you meet my needs." "I love you" comes to mean no more than "you scratch my itch." That kind of love too is destined for tragedy, because it turns the person I love into a means for meeting my needs, a means for my own gratification. That is a lie about the person loved, and it is a perversion of the true nature of love. It is a form of self-idolatry, because it says that the person I love exists to satisfy me.

An opposite tendency can also lead to tragedy. Instead of using the one I love for my own purposes, I can renounce any interest in or and claim upon the one I love. True love within this view means giving the beloved complete freedom from all demands and commitment. No strings, no ties, no claims, no expectations, no future. This too is quite common in our day, with its free-floating, noncommittal premarital relations. Such a love is inherently tragic because it is not love at all. No true lover can be indifferent to the response of his beloved. Every lover makes a claim on his beloved. Every lover wants to stake out some sort of ownership. Every lover wants to say of his beloved, "She is mine." Every woman wants to say the same of her lover.

When we put these points together, we have the first clue to avoiding marital tragedy. On the one hand, love always makes claims. Dan has shown his love for Jessica by asking her to marry him, by seeking to make a claim on her time, attention, resources, body, and person. By answering "yes," Jessica is accepting Dan's claims on her and is also staking claims of her own. Dan, you can say "Jessica is *my* wife," and Jessica, you can say "Dan is *my* husband." But, on the other hand, true love never makes total claims. True love always recognizes that there is something more to the beloved than the lover can claim. If you truly love, you'll recognize that your beloved does not exist to satisfy you. Dan, Jessica is yours, but not only yours; Jessica, you have claims on Dan, but you are not the only one who has claims on him. True Christian love always recognizes that there is a Divine Lover who also makes claims and who always has prior ownership.

Among Christians, to say that marriages always involve three is a cliché, but it is far more than a cliché. It is part of the very structure of an enduring marriage and, in fact, the very structure of love. If a marriage is to work without collapsing tragically into mutual self-gratification or mutual indifference, it must be more than a joining of two. There must be a Third, and His claims and demands must be ultimate.

There is yet another reason why contemporary love and contemporary marriage so often end tragically. Understood as a feeling, natural impulse, or instinct, love resists structure, resists constraint, and resists "artifice." For many today, marriage itself is one of the constraints that must be resisted and abandoned; marriage is artificial and must melt before the heat of naked passion. Living together is natural and hence good; random sex is natural and hence good; marriage is artificial and therefore bad.

This is a misunderstanding of love in a basic way. Artifice is always the first product of love. When Adam first saw Eve, he spoke the first recorded words of a human being, and it is a small poem: "She is bone of my bones, and flesh of my flesh; she shall be called woman, for she was taken from man." Ever since, men have been composing poems in praise of women, and when they don't compose poetry, they seek other, equally artificial ways to impress women.

Love always produces art—that is, love always produces artifice. A lover always behaves in unnatural ways.

This applies not only to individual lovers but also to whole cultures. Courtship and marriage have always been governed by a code of behavior that dictates how lovers are to approach one another. Fifty years ago, a young man would talk with a young woman on a porch swing; today, she invites him out for a beer or a movie. The conventions have changed, but there still are conventions. Paradoxically, when it comes to love, nothing is more natural than artifice.[1]

Ignoring or denying the necessity of artifice—of constraints, of "unnatural" structures and practices—leads to disaster. Unless it is given shape by a code of conduct, a tradition of courtship, and the structure of marriage, love is again reduced to mere desire or impulse. Love is again reduced to something short-lived, ephemeral, vaporous. Without the artifice of marriage, love must end in tragedy.

In fact, of course, marriage is not artificial. It is not a product of culture or human invention. It is a divine institution, invented by God for the first man and first woman in the Garden of Eden. And here we have a second clue to avoiding tragedy in marriage. It involves recognizing that this ceremony and gathering is not merely traditional. This ceremony takes place in the presence of God, and the making of this covenant is witnessed not only by the friends and family gathered here, but also by the Father of our Lord Jesus Christ.

This means that the marriage vows you will both take in a few moments are vows that will be taken in the presence of God. Throughout Scripture, vows and oaths of this kind are self-maledictory. That is, you are swearing on pain of curses and death that you will do as you promise. Dan, you

---

[1] Some of these thoughts were inspired by Peter Saccio's lectures on Shakespeare, available from The Teaching Company.

are swearing in God's holy name that you will love Jessica as Christ loved His church, giving His own life for her sake. Jessica, you are swearing in God's holy name that you will submit to, honor, and obey your husband, as the church to Christ. This is the covenant you are making today, and this is not a game. This is not mere human invention, mere tradition, mere artifice. This is divine artifice, God's art, the product of the Lord's love for His bride.

Many marriages today end in tragedy, but marriage need not end in tragedy. Tragedy is not built into the fabric of things. One of the basic affirmations of the Christian faith, and one reflected in the text from Revelation 21, is that the world will end in a wedding that leads to a marriage in which every vestige of tragedy and sorrow is removed—a marriage without tears, death, mourning, or pain. Endings reveal the truth of things, and the end of *all* things reveals that the human drama is not a tragedy but a comedy.

Your marriage, like everything in this life, will be marked by loss, tears, and difficulties. But that does not mean that your marriage must be tragic. With faith in the Husband of the church, looking forward with hope to this final and perfect wedding, your marriage can be a sign and a foretaste of the joy of that marriage. The end of your marriage, which will reveal the truth of your marriage, can be an anticipation of the end of all things. And only by such faith, hope, and love can the end of your marriage fulfill the joy of its beginning.

In the name of the Father, and of the Son, and of the Holy Spirit. Amen.

14 BEAUTY BEYOND THE WEDDING DAY

Marriage of Joshua and Sara Appel
June 5, 2004

SCRIPTURE READING

Revelation 21:2
>And I saw the holy city, new Jerusalem, coming down out of heaven from God, made ready as a bride adorned for her husband.

HOMILY

Weddings are beautiful, and few events are more so: the silken cascade of the bride's dress, the sanctuary warm with candlelight, the austere elegance of a black tuxedo, the dignified choreography of procession and recession, and the indescribable transcendence of Holst's "Jupiter" straining to burst the space of the sanctuary.

Weddings are beautiful, and therefore weddings also evoke beauty. Something there is about a wedding that inspires beauty—that inspires art, music, poetry. What went on in the last frantic weeks before this wedding was not merely an effort to make the wedding beautiful. Love is always already a collaborative work of art: two lives pursuing harmonization, two independent lines reaching for rhyme, two relatively unformed persons molding one another, a man and a woman learning to dance in a single movement. As celebrations and formalizations of love, weddings do not need to be made beautiful; they are beautiful. Our preparations are efforts to make that beauty more visible, audible, and tangible.

And, beyond this, the frantic preparations were a response to the unimagined beauty of that wedding that we see distantly before us, as through a glass darkly. Every wedding radiates with the glory of the final wedding that John glimpsed in vision. As with all art, the art of a wedding and the art of love involve a bestowal of beauty, because they are first responses to beauty.

In his poem "Prothalamion," Edmund Spenser describes a splendid wedding. He imagines the bride and groom as stately swans swimming down the Thames, greeted by troops of nymphs strewing flowers in the river. Of the nymphs, he wrote:

> Seemed they never saw a sight so fair,
> Of fowls so lovely that they sure did deem
> Them heavenly born . . .
> For sure they did not seem
> To be begot of any earthly seed,
> But rather angels, or of angels' breed;
> Yet were they bred of summer's-heat, they say,
> In sweetest season, when each flower and weed
> The earth did fresh array,
> So fresh they seemed as day,
> Even as their bridal day, which was not long:
> Sweet Thames run softly, till I end my song.

Weddings are beautiful, but too many marriages are not. Surveying the wasteland of modern life, love, and marriage, T. S. Eliot subverted Spenser's vision of an unearthly wedding. He wrote in *The Waste Land,*

> The nymphs are departed.
> Sweet Thames, run softly, till I end my song.
> The river bears no empty bottles, sandwich papers,
> Silk handkerchiefs, cardboard boxes, cigarette ends

Or other testimony of summer nights. The nymphs are
  departed.
And their friends, the loitering heirs of city directors;
Departed, have left no addresses. . . .
Sweet Thames, run softly till I end my song,
Sweet Thames, run softly, for I speak not loud or long.

Marriages that begin in beauty may degenerate into endless bickering, long and silent resentments, incessant re-
criminations and reprisals, and finally the wrenching death
of divorce. Few events are more spectacular than a celebrity wedding, but few are more pathetic than the often pro-
tracted and always public decay of a celebrity marriage.
Dying is always ugly, and the death of a marriage is always
at least a double death. As Eliot said, for many today "the
nymphs are departed." How does this happen? How do
marriages that begin with beauty end in ugliness?

Some marriages, paradoxically, end in ugliness because
of an overvaluation of beauty itself. We are constantly told
by our culture—in films, romantic novels, and advertisements—that beauty of a particular kind is a sound basis,
and perhaps the only sound basis, for lasting love. As Robert Solomon has pointed out, the problem with this perspective is not so much that that beauty is superficial. In an important sense, beauty is more than "skin-deep"; it reveals
character, because how we "make ourselves up" tells a great
deal about what we want to "make of ourselves." Rather,
the primary problem is that the glamorous beauty promoted
in advertising and film "points in precisely the [wrong] direction for love—toward admiration and worship rather
than sharing, toward arousal instead of wisdom, toward superficial attraction rather than deep intimacy and knowledge." Beauty "attracts," but "'attraction' presupposes a
distance, a distance which the intimacy of love denies."[1]

---

[1] Robert Solomon, *About Love: Reinventing Romance for our
Times* (New York: Touchstone/Simon & Schuster, 1989).

What passes for beauty today is often vain, childish, narcissistic, and what attracts is less the seductiveness of beauty than a certain condescending attitude of unavailability, and unavailability is the very antithesis of love.

Idolization of beauty often takes another form as well. A man shops for a wife—or, a woman picks out a man—as an attractive adornment, an appendage, a trophy. Couples may choose a lifestyle—the best home in the best neighborhood, the latest model car, a perfectly manicured lawn, the right clubs, and the right friends—for the sole purpose of impressing others with the elegance of their lifestyle. Living and loving, including the living and loving of marriage, becomes a display. Such aestheticism is an enemy to life. Instead of living, aesthetes of this sort stand to the side examining their lives, barking instructions like a film director, adding a dash of color here, smoothing off a rough piece of stone there. Such aestheticism has little to do with living, and this kind of self-display has nothing at all to do with Christian living.

Christians are rarely in danger of making the mistakes I've outlined, although we are never above temptation of any sort. But Christians today are much more in danger of making another kind of mistake that has remarkably similar results. Many Christians consider beauty to be irrelevant for life and marriage, tolerable for the wedding day but dispensable for the rest of life. That too is a prescription for an ugly marriage following a beautiful wedding.

The pursuit of beauty in the proper sense is intimately conjoined with the pursuit of holiness, because the God we worship and serve is beautiful and is Beauty. Joshua and Sara, this afternoon I want to remind you of things you have already embraced with enthusiasm, things you have included in the blueprint of your life together. This afternoon I want to remind you that you must persevere in these things if you hope to make your marriage as lovely as your wedding.

First, live in wisdom. Now what has wisdom to do with beauty? Much in every way. Wisdom, of course, involves prudence, practicality, and common sense, but in Scripture wisdom also includes an irreducible aesthetic element. The Hebrew word for wisdom means "skill," and it can be used to describe craftsmanship, as it does in the case of Bezalel and Oholiab, who were given wisdom to construct the furnishings of the tabernacle. When applied to life, the word does not lose its aesthetic, artistic, or craft dimension. Living wisely means living artfully.

Wisdom is often an issue of "fittingness," and this is an aesthetic criterion. The right words at the right time are not only ethically good and rationally sound, but are also "like apples of gold in a setting of silver" (Prov. 25:11), which is to say, fitting words are beautiful. In your marriage you will quickly learn, if you have not already, how damaging unfitting words can be. And the criterion of fittingness applies to actions as much as to words. Bringing a bouquet of flowers at the wrong time can seem like an attack, whatever your motives. Doing the right thing at the right time is wisdom, and this wisdom is a form of craftsmanship, learned over a lifetime of training.

Wisdom, the Proverbs tell us further, is better than silver, gold, and precious jewels—it is not only more valuable but also more beautiful. Wisdom is a beautiful woman, and Lady Wisdom offers to adorn with a crown of beauty those who find her. It is no accident that the same Solomon who wrote many of the Proverbs also wrote the Song of Songs, for this erotic poem too is about the desire for wisdom, which is finally also the desire for beauty. Joshua and Sara: Live in wisdom. Live in the fear of the Lord, for the fear of the Lord is the beginning of wisdom, and the beginning of beauty.

Second, live in hope. What has hope to do with beauty? Much in every way. To live in hope is to live toward the future, desiring and expecting God to fulfill His promises. All the hope we have as Christians is fundamentally a hope for beauty. God created Adam and Eve in glory and splendor, but they sinned and fell short of the glory of God. All of us have also fallen short of God's glory, but the great hope of the gospel is a hope for restored glory. We see and know and experience present glory only as a participation in future glory. The glory of your marriage will be evident only if it is an anticipation of the glory of the union of Christ and His church in the marriage feast of the Last Day.

To live in hope is to live toward the future, and this has very concrete implications for your marriage. One of the most debilitating habits in marriage is the stubborn refusal to leave the past behind and move toward a new future. Yesterday's unthinking criticism hangs like the shadow of death over today and endless tomorrows; last year's forgotten anniversary poisons every future anniversary; sins unforgiven and unforgotten lend their darkly discordant overtones to every conversation. You can have a happy marriage only through ready confession of sin, continual forgiveness, repeated reconciliations, and unwavering forbearance and gentleness. You can achieve a beautiful marriage only by following Paul's instructions to "be kind to one another, tender-hearted, forgiving each other, just as God in Christ also has forgiven you" (Eph. 4:32). Forgiveness is always a turning from past sin to future glory; forgiveness is the concrete expression of hope, a hope for final reconciliation, a hope of beauty. Joshua and Sara: Live in hope, live in the hope of glory, so that future glory might be expressed in your marriage.

Finally, live in faith. What has faith to do with beauty? Much in every way. Faith always arises from despair of your own resources and options. Faith is, as Paul said of Abraham's faith, hope against hope. Faith is hope in God that competes with and finally defeats hopelessness in ourselves. Faith means trusting God to work in us so that we may work out our salvation with fear and trembling. Faith is openness and surrender to God's work in, with, and through us. Faith is ecstasy, joyfully taking one's stand outside oneself, in God.

We are glorified by faith as much as we are justified and sanctified through faith. The God who works in us is the original, the infinite Beauty, and we rely on Him to display that beauty in us. God's very being is "love, [the Father's] delight in the glorious radiance of his infinite Image, seen in the boundlessly lovely light of his Spirit." And creation, according to David Hart's summary of Gregory of Nyssa, "is a symphonic and rhythmic complication of diversity, motion and rest, a song praising God, [who is] the true, primordial, archetypal music, in which human nature can glimpse itself as in a mirror." We are, in short, "music moved to music."[2] Faith means trusting God to play His infinite fugue through our finite lives, to sing His eternal song in our temporality, to transpose the harmonious polyphony that is His uncreated life into the key of created existence.

And He does do exactly that. Our limitations and sins are no limitations for Him. Gregory compares the soul that receives God's blessings "to a vessel endlessly expanding as it receives what flows into it inexhaustibly." Receiving God's beauty in faith makes us "ever more capacious and receptive of beauty."[3] So it will be with your marriage, if it is grounded in faith—your individual faith and your faith together. Joshua and Sara: Live in faith, trusting God to play out His eternal song with ever-increasing vibrancy through the harmony of your marriage.

Live in wisdom, together as you have separately; live in hope, as man and wife; live in faith, as two made one flesh. Then your marriage will be beautiful, progressively transformed from glory to glory, from beauty to beauty, and it

---

[2] David Bentley Hart, *The Beauty of the Infinite* (Grand Rapids: Eerdmans, 2003).

[3] Ibid.

will continually and increasingly display the splendor not only of your wedding day, but also the splendor of the Endless God who will unveil Himself in the Endless day, which is also a wedding day.

In the Name of the Father, and of the Son, and of the Holy Spirit. Amen.